LEARNING

TO

LEAD

Essential Attributes Of Effective Leadership

William W. Walker

Table of Contents

Introduction

It was only after considerable and thoughtful deliberation that I made the decision to publish this book. In the realm of leadership education and business consulting, it is my view that originality is exceedingly rare. This publication does not claim to deviate from that perspective.

It may appear unconventional for an author to introduce a work, which they earnestly hope will aid you in mastering the extensive skills that constitute the broad concept of leadership, with such modesty. However, it is important to set the expectation that this book does not contain novel concepts. Indeed, if the primary motive behind acquiring this book was the anticipation of discovering groundbreaking insights into leadership that have not been encountered in your previous experiential and educational pursuits, I must caution that you may find yourself disappointed.

The primary objective behind the creation of this book was not predicated on the notion that I possessed novel insights previously undiscovered in the domain of leadership. Instead, my goal was to curate and present ten fundamental qualities and attributes of effective leadership, offering a framework or blueprint for those committed to the rigorous process of skill enhancement. The term 'blueprint' is deliberately chosen to describe this framework. It is crucial to understand that this book does not serve as a step-by-step manual with explicit instructions guaranteeing the realization of a finished product. Much like an architectural blueprint that outlines the "what" and the "where" for tradespeople without dictating the exact "how", this book similarly sets the framework without prescribing specific methodologies. The complexities of individual realities preclude this. At this juncture, I wish to propose the most effective utilization of this text, from the perspective of its humble author.

Should I have the privilege of presenting this book to a business leader who would derive value from its contents, my recommendation for the "how" would entail the following approach:

1. Engage in a thorough reading of the book from beginning to end.
2. Revisit the first chapter, initiating a detailed second reading.
3. Dedicate yourself to *daily* re-readings of this initial chapter until you achieve a robust conceptual grasp and have effectively incorporated its principles into your daily routines. The duration required for this step could span from a few weeks to several months, or even years, depending on individual progress.
4. Refrain from progressing to the subsequent chapter until the mastery and practical application of the current chapter's content are fully realized.
5. Methodically apply these steps to each chapter, ensuring the comprehensive assimilation of all critical leadership attributes delineated in this book.

As I pen these words, I am aware that only a select few, if any, will embrace the challenge I propose. For those contemplating this undertaking, I pose the following question: Over the past year, how many books on leadership have you perused? Two? Five? Perhaps ten? From these readings, can you identify a single concept that you have consistently applied to your daily practices for a duration exceeding 90 days? More critically, are you able to recognize any skills from your readings that have become seamlessly integrated into your leadership approach? While numerous individuals might affirm the former, it is anticipated that only a scarce few will affirm the latter.

These observations do not diminish the value that can be extracted by individuals seeking an engaging read or affirmation of their current leadership trajectory. Indeed, there is significant merit accessible within these pages for any leader in pursuit of insight. Furthermore, it is conceivable that I might have articulated certain concepts in a manner uniquely resonant, perhaps presenting ideas in a light previously unencountered by the reader. My intention is not to dissuade you from proceeding with this book; on the contrary, I am genuinely appreciative that this work has found its way to you.

As you navigate the intricate landscape of business in your esteemed role as a practitioner of leadership, it is essential to acknowledge that this text does not offer a universal solution or a panacea for mastering the integration of the pivotal attributes discussed. The complexities and variances inherent in our individual daily professional responsibilities preclude a one-size-fits-all approach. However, for those who are prepared to invest the time and effort, this book provides a comprehensive blueprint.

This blueprint is designed for the diligent leader who is ready to engage in a transformative process, one that requires a deliberate deceleration and a commitment to deep, introspective work. The journey outlined within these pages is not a quick fix but an illumination of the path toward profound personal and professional growth. By following the guidance provided, you have the opportunity to construct a version of yourself that is markedly distinct and more refined than the individual who first turned these pages.

This evolution demands not just the acquisition of knowledge but the application and integration of these leadership attributes into your daily practices. It is an endeavor that calls for persistence, resilience, and an unwavering dedication to self-improvement. For those who are willing to undertake this rigorous journey, the rewards are substantial. You will emerge not only as a more effective leader but as an individual who embodies the principles of leadership in every action and decision.

In embracing this challenge, you set forth on a path that not only enhances your capabilities as a leader but also elevates the standard of leadership within your sphere of influence. The blueprint laid out in this book is a starting point, a guide to building a legacy of leadership that is both impactful and enduring. It is an invitation to create a future where the leader you become is a beacon of inspiration and excellence, fundamentally different and more evolved than the version of yourself that embarked on this journey.

1.Vision

Among the dynamic collection of attributes and skills that intertwine to form the embodiment of effective leadership, the concept of vision holds a place of paramount importance, acting as the linchpin that secures the trajectory of both individuals and organizations towards realms of success yet uncharted. Vision transcends the immediacy of operational objectives to encapsulate a broader, more aspirational horizon. It is not merely about setting targets but about forging a legacy, crafting a dynamic blueprint that ignites action, fosters motivation, and catalyzes change.

At its core, vision in leadership embodies a forward-looking perspective, a clear and compelling picture of what the future could be. Unlike goals, which are specific, measurable, and often short-term, vision is expansive and boundless, capturing the imagination and stirring the soul. It is a profound statement of intent that distinguishes transformative leaders from mere managers. This distinction is crucial, as it highlights the visionary leader's role not just in steering the organization towards predefined outcomes but in crafting a narrative that inspires collective action and dedication.

A vision, in this context, is a beacon of aspiration that goes beyond the mundane confines of routine operations. It is the articulation of a desired future that reflects the highest aspirations of the organization and its members. It is both a destination and a journey, providing a sense of purpose and direction while also allowing for innovation and adaptation along the way. The development of such a vision requires a deep understanding of the organization's core values, its strengths, and the opportunities and challenges that lie ahead. It also demands a keen sense of empathy and insight into the aspirations and needs of those the organization serves.

To fully grasp the significance of vision in leadership, it is essential to differentiate it from related concepts such as missions and objectives. A mission statement defines the organization's purpose, its reason for existing. It is often focused on the present, outlining the fundamental services or products provided. Objectives, on the other hand, are specific, measurable targets set to achieve strategic goals. They are the steps an organization takes to realize its mission.

Vision, by contrast, is inherently future-oriented and aspirational. It paints a picture of the future the organization seeks to create, serving as a source of inspiration and motivation. While missions and objectives are critical for operational success, vision is what propels an organization towards transformative change. It is the dream that fuels innovation, the aspiration that drives excellence.

2

A well-articulated vision acts as an indispensable compass, offering direction and purpose amidst the fluctuating dynamics of organizational life. It stands as a constant, a north star guiding the collective efforts of the organization. In this capacity, vision ensures that every decision and action is aligned with the overarching aspirations, mitigating the risk of deviation from core values and strategic objectives.

The analogy of the vision as a compass is particularly apt in the context of leadership, as it emphasizes the need for orientation and guidance. Just as a compass provides direction to a traveler in unfamiliar territory, a vision offers a path forward in the complex and often unpredictable landscape of organizational life. It helps leaders and their teams navigate challenges, seize opportunities, and make decisions that are coherent with the long-term aspirations of the organization.

One of the critical functions of a vision is to harmonize the organization's resources and strategies toward achieving shared aspirations. In the absence of a clear vision, resources can be squandered, and efforts can become fragmented. A vision serves as a unifying force, aligning strategies, and ensuring that resources are deployed efficiently and effectively towards the common goal.

This alignment is crucial in today's fast-paced and competitive environment. Organizations face an array of challenges, from technological disruptions to shifting market dynamics. A clear and compelling vision helps to focus efforts, prioritize initiatives, and ensure

3

that the organization remains agile and responsive to change. It fosters a culture of strategic thinking, where decisions are made with an eye toward the future.

One of the key aspects of vision in the context of leadership is its capacity to foster a collective journey toward achieving shared aspirations. A vision is not just a leader's dream; it is a shared aspiration that resonates with the values and hopes of the entire organization. It is a call to action that invites every member of the organization to contribute their unique talents and energies towards a common purpose.

This sense of collective endeavor is critical to the success of any organization. It builds a sense of community and belonging, fostering a culture of collaboration and mutual support. When individuals feel connected to a shared vision, they are more likely to go above and beyond, to innovate, and to strive for excellence. A vision thus serves as a powerful motivator, inspiring individuals to contribute their best towards the realization of the collective dream.

Another vital function of vision in leadership is its role in mitigating the risk of deviation from core values and strategic objectives. In the absence of a clear vision, organizations can easily be sidetracked by short-term gains or distracted by emerging challenges. A vision provides a framework for decision-making, ensuring that every choice is

4

evaluated in the context of its contribution to the long-term aspirations of the organization.

This strategic alignment is essential for maintaining the integrity and coherence of the organization's efforts. It ensures that the organization remains true to its values and objectives, even in the face of adversity. By keeping the vision at the forefront of decision-making, leaders can navigate the complexities of organizational life with confidence and clarity.

Shaping Culture

Vision serves as the cornerstone of an organization's identity, influencing its values, norms, and behaviors. It is the guiding light that directs the organization's operations and interactions, both internally and externally. The crafting of culture through vision is a dynamic process, spearheaded by leaders who embody and communicate the vision to every member of the organization.

At the heart of every organization's culture lies its vision—a clear and compelling depiction of what the organization aspires to achieve. This vision is not merely a statement of goals or objectives; it is a declaration of the organization's purpose and values. It answers the fundamental questions of why the organization exists and what it stands

5

for. As such, the vision is a critical tool for leaders in shaping the organizational culture.

Culture, in essence, is the sum of the shared values, norms, and behaviors that characterize an organization. It is the unwritten code that governs how people in the organization interact with each other and with the external world. The process of shaping this culture begins with the articulation of a vision that reflects the organization's core values and aspirations. When effectively communicated and embodied by leadership, this vision becomes the foundation upon which the organizational culture is built.

The first step in molding organizational culture through vision is its effective communication. Leaders must ensure that the vision is not only communicated clearly and consistently but also in a manner that resonates with the members of the organization. This involves not just verbal communication but also the leader's actions, decisions, and the systems and processes established within the organization. When the vision is communicated in a way that connects with the individuals' values and aspirations, it fosters a sense of ownership and commitment to the vision across the organization.

For a vision to truly shape culture, there must be alignment between the organization's stated values and the actual behaviors of its members. Leaders play a critical role in ensuring this alignment by modeling the behaviors that reflect the vision and values of the

6

organization. They also need to recognize and reward behaviors that align with the vision while addressing behaviors that do not. This alignment process is continuous and requires leaders to be actively engaged in nurturing the culture they wish to see in their organization.

Vision influences organizational culture by guiding decision-making processes. When a clear vision is in place, decisions are made with a long-term perspective, considering the organization's ultimate goals. This fosters a culture of strategic thinking and prudent risk-taking. The vision acts as a criterion for evaluating options and making choices, ensuring that decisions are consistent with the organization's values and objectives. This strategic alignment reinforces the culture by embedding the vision into the daily operations and decision-making frameworks of the organization.

The influence of a well-defined vision on interpersonal relationships and team dynamics is profound. A shared vision fosters a sense of unity and collaboration among team members. It encourages open communication, mutual respect, and support, as individuals work together towards a common goal. The vision provides a sense of purpose that transcends individual interests, promoting a culture of teamwork and collective achievement. Leaders can cultivate this collaborative environment by encouraging team-based projects and initiatives that align with the vision, thereby strengthening interpersonal bonds and team cohesion within the organization.

7

While the role of vision in crafting culture is critical, it is not without challenges. Ensuring that the vision permeates every aspect of the organization and truly influences its culture requires persistent effort and commitment. Leaders may face resistance to change, misalignments between stated values and actual behaviors, and challenges in communicating the vision in a way that resonates with all members of the organization. Overcoming these challenges involves continuous engagement with the team, reinforcement of the vision and values, and a commitment to embodying the vision in every action and decision.

Organizations that have successfully leveraged vision to shape their culture can provide valuable insights. Companies like Google, with its vision of organizing the world's information and making it universally accessible and useful, have fostered a culture of innovation and continuous improvement. Non-profit organizations like the World Wildlife Fund, with a vision of building a future where people live in harmony with nature, have cultivated a culture of conservation and sustainability. These tenets are interwoven into the fabric of what these companies represent, allowing them to attract and recruit top-tier, like-minded talent which drives innovation and progress. These examples illustrate how a well-articulated and embodied vision can guide cultural evolution, driving organizational success.

Through effective communication, alignment of values and behaviors, strategic decision-making, and fostering positive interpersonal relationships, leaders can mold the culture to reflect the organization's vision. While challenges may arise, the potential for vision to transform organizational culture is immense. As leaders commit to embodying and reinforcing the vision, they pave the way for a culture that not only aligns with the organization's goals but also inspires and motivates its members to achieve greatness.

Aligning Individual Goals

The profound impact of a leader's vision on both individual and collective goals within an organization is a testament to the transformative power of visionary leadership. This intricate interplay between a shared vision and personal aspirations not only aligns efforts toward achieving common objectives but also fosters an environment where individual team members find personal fulfillment and motivation. It transcends the boundaries of mere operational targets to embody the core values and purpose of the organization, thereby serving as a powerful motivator and unifier for the team. The essence of this dynamic lies in the ability of a well-articulated vision to resonate deeply with individuals, inspiring them to elevate their performance and contribute meaningfully to the collective journey of organizational success.

The alignment of an organization's vision with the personal goals of its members is fundamental to the realization of this vision. This alignment is not coincidental but requires deliberate action and communication by leaders. It involves understanding the diverse motivations, strengths, and aspirations of team members and demonstrating how the vision provides a pathway for individual growth and achievement.

Leaders must engage in active dialogue with their team members to understand their personal goals and motivations. This understanding allows leaders to tailor their approach to communicating the vision, making it relevant and inspiring to each individual. When team members see how their personal aspirations align with the organization's vision, they are more likely to commit themselves fully to its realization.

A key aspect of aligning vision with individual goals is the emphasis on personal growth and development. Visionary leaders create opportunities for learning, skill development, and career advancement within the framework of the vision's objectives. By investing in their team's development, leaders not only advance the organization's capabilities but also demonstrate a commitment to the individual well-being and success of their members.

The relationship between a leader's vision and individual performance is characterized by a reciprocal dynamic, where the pursuit of the vision enhances individual performance, and in turn, elevated individual performance drives the organization closer to its vision. A compelling vision acts as a catalyst for elevating individual performance. It provides clarity of purpose and direction, allowing team members to focus their efforts on activities that contribute to the vision. This clarity reduces ambiguity and inefficiency, enabling individuals to work with a sense of purpose and urgency. Moreover, the inspiration derived from a shared vision fosters creativity, innovation, and a willingness to take calculated risks, all of which are essential for high performance and organizational advancement.

The collective achievement of the organization's vision is the culmination of the individual contributions of its members. Each team member's efforts and achievements add up to create momentum towards realizing the vision. The synergistic effect of aligned individual goals and collective objectives ensures that the organization moves forward cohesively and effectively. This collective success, in turn, reinforces the individual's sense of accomplishment and connection to the vision, creating a positive feedback loop that perpetuates motivation and engagement.

Examining real-life examples of organizations where visionary leadership has successfully aligned individual aspirations with the collective vision can provide valuable insights into the practical application of these principles. These case studies reveal common themes, such as the importance of clear communication, the role of the

11

leader as coach and mentor, and the need for an organizational culture that values and supports personal growth.

For instance, in companies known for their innovative cultures, leaders often set ambitious visions that challenge the status quo. Elon Musk, Jeff Bezos, Muhammad Yunus; These visionaries act as a magnet for individuals who share a passion for innovation and a desire to make a significant impact. Through shared interests and initiatives that encourage experimentation, learning, and the sharing of ideas, these organizations not only advance toward their visionary goals but also foster an environment where individuals can pursue their personal aspirations of creativity and discovery.

Aligning individual goals with the organization's vision is not without its challenges. Diverse individual aspirations, varying levels of engagement, and resistance to change can all hinder the alignment process. Visionary leaders must therefore be adept at navigating these challenges through effective communication, inclusive decision-making, and fostering a culture of trust and transparency.

Clear, consistent communication is crucial in aligning individual and collective goals. Leaders must articulate the vision in a way that is understandable and resonates with team members. This includes sharing the rationale behind the vision, how it was developed, and the role each team member plays in its realization. Regular updates on

12

progress towards the vision also help maintain alignment and motivation.

Involving team members in decision-making processes related to the vision's implementation fosters a sense of ownership and commitment. When individuals feel their input is valued and that they have a stake in the outcome, they are more likely to align their personal goals with the organization's objectives.

Trust and transparency are foundational to the successful alignment of vision and individual goals. Leaders must build trust by being open about challenges, acknowledging contributions, and being consistent in their actions and decisions. A transparent culture where feedback is encouraged and valued further strengthens the alignment by ensuring that any misalignments are addressed promptly and effectively.

A well-articulated vision not only aligns efforts towards a common objective but also resonates with individual aspirations, elevating performance and fulfillment. Through understanding individual motivations, fostering personal growth, and navigating the challenges of alignment, visionary leaders can harness the full potential of their teams. The result is a dynamic organization where the pursuit of a shared vision leads to both individual and collective achievements, embodying the true essence of visionary leadership.

Summary

The profound impact of a clear and compelling vision becomes clear through the lens of serving as a beacon, guiding organizations through the complexities of the modern business environment, and providing a sense of purpose that supersedes

day-to-day activities. Visionary leadership is at the heart of this dynamic, bridging the gap between the organization's broad objectives and the personal aspirations of its members. This intricate interplay between the individual and the collective within the framework of visionary leadership illuminates the path to not just organizational success but also personal fulfillment and growth for every team member involved.

Visionary leadership involves the cultivation of an environment where every member feels their contributions are both valued and vital to the collective journey. This culture of inclusivity and respect is pivotal in aligning individual aspirations with the organization's overarching objectives. When team members see their personal goals reflected in the broader vision, their engagement and motivation soar, driving them to contribute their best efforts toward the realization of shared objectives. This alignment is not a static state but a dynamic process that requires continuous nurturing and adaptation by visionary leaders.

14

The symbiotic relationship fostered between individual aspirations and the organizational vision leads to a multitude of benefits. On an individual level, it promotes a sense of ownership and accountability, as team members recognize their role in the broader narrative of the organization's journey. This sense of belonging and purpose is instrumental in fostering personal growth and fulfillment, as individuals are motivated to develop their skills and contribute more significantly to the collective effort.

On an organizational level, the integration of diverse strengths and goals under a unified vision propels the organization towards unprecedented heights of achievement. The collective effort of a team, aligned in purpose and direction, is a powerful force capable of overcoming challenges, driving innovation, and achieving strategic objectives. This collaborative environment, nurtured by visionary leadership, becomes a crucible for innovation, as diverse ideas and perspectives merge to create novel solutions and approaches.

Moreover, the pursuit of a shared vision under the guidance of visionary leadership does more than just achieve immediate objectives; it lays the foundation for a legacy of innovation, excellence, and meaningful impact. Organizations that succeed in aligning the individual aspirations of their members with their overarching vision become beacons in their respective industries, setting new standards and pushing the boundaries of what is possible. They create environments

15

where innovation thrives, excellence is the norm, and the impact of their work resonates well beyond their immediate sphere of influence.

The role of a visionary leader in aligning individual and collective goals under a shared vision is a critical driver of organizational success and personal fulfillment. By fostering a culture that values and integrates the diverse strengths and aspirations of its team members, organizations can unlock the full potential of their collective efforts. This alignment not only propels the organization and its members towards achieving their objectives but also creates a lasting legacy of innovation, excellence, and impact. In the journey towards mastering the skills of effective leadership, the clear articulation of a shared vision stands as the cornerstone, guiding both the organization and its members towards a future marked by achievement and meaningful contribution.

2.Communication

Effective communication is an attribute of effective leadership and a fundamental element that transcends the mere exchange of information to become a pivotal force in shaping organizational culture, driving team cohesion, and achieving strategic goals. Improving our leadership effectiveness requires exploration into the intricacies of communication within the leadership context, unraveling how clarity, persuasiveness, active listening, and feedback integration not only enhance the transmission of ideas but also fortify the bonds of trust, openness, and mutual respect essential for any successful leadership endeavor.

At its core, effective communication embodies the deliberate and strategic sharing of ideas, expectations, and visions in a manner that is both clear and compelling. It involves a two-way exchange where not only is information conveyed, but feedback is also solicited and valued. This dynamic process is fundamental in aligning team efforts with organizational objectives, thereby facilitating the realization of a leader's vision.

Clarity in communication is paramount. Leaders must articulate their thoughts and directives in a manner that is unambiguous and

18

straightforward, leaving no room for misinterpretation. This clarity of message ensures that team members are fully aware of what is expected of them, the goals they are working towards, and the standards by which their performance is measured. The precision of language, the simplicity of the message, and the relevance of the content all contribute to the effectiveness of the communication process.

Communication in a leadership context is a skill that requires one to exceed the simple dissemination of information to embody the persuasive conveyance of ideas and strategies. It's about inspiring action, influencing decision-making, and motivating teams to embrace and work towards a shared vision. Persuasiveness in communication is not about manipulation but about presenting ideas in a compelling manner that resonates with the values, needs, and aspirations of the team. It involves the strategic use of rhetoric, storytelling, and emotional intelligence to engage and mobilize followers.

Effective communication is inherently a two-way process. Active listening is as crucial as articulate speaking. Leaders must demonstrate a genuine interest in the ideas, concerns, and feedback of their team members. This involves not just hearing but understanding the underlying messages, reading non-verbal cues, and acknowledging the contributions of others. Active listening fosters an environment of trust and respect, where team members feel valued and understood. It

19

enhances team dynamics, facilitates conflict resolution, and encourages a culture of open dialogue and collaboration.

The integration of feedback is a critical component of effective leadership communication. Leaders must not only solicit feedback but also act upon it, demonstrating adaptability and a commitment to continuous improvement. This feedback loop reinforces the value placed on team members' input, empowering them and fostering a sense of ownership over collective outcomes. It allows for the adjustment of strategies, the clarification of objectives, and the refinement of processes, thereby enhancing the team's ability to achieve its goals.

At the heart of effective leadership lies the trust between leaders and their followers. Clear, honest, and open communication is essential in building and sustaining this trust. When leaders communicate transparently about their vision, challenges, and the rationale behind decisions, they build credibility and integrity. Trust is further reinforced when leaders actively listen to and act upon feedback, demonstrating respect for their team members' perspectives and contributions.

Effective communication fosters a sense of unity and purpose among team members. By clearly articulating a shared vision and ensuring that each member understands their role in achieving collective objectives, leaders can enhance team cohesion and collaboration. Open channels of communication encourage the sharing of ideas, fostering innovation, and creativity. Active listening and feedback integration further enhance teamwork by ensuring that all voices are heard and valued, promoting a culture of inclusivity and mutual support.

In times of change, communication becomes even more critical. Leaders must effectively convey the need for change, the benefits it will bring, and the steps required to achieve it. Persuasive communication can motivate teams to embrace change, while active listening allows leaders to address concerns and resistance, facilitating a smoother transition. By integrating feedback and adapting strategies as needed, leaders can guide their organizations through change, minimizing disruptions and maintaining focus on long-term objectives.

Effective communication enhances decision-making and problem-solving by ensuring that all relevant information is shared and considered. Clarity in communication ensures that team members have a comprehensive understanding of the issues at hand, while active listening and feedback integration bring diverse perspectives and ideas to the table. This collaborative approach to decision-making leverages the collective expertise of the team, leading to more informed, innovative, and effective solutions.

Crafting The Message

In the world of leadership, the ability to craft clear and persuasive messages is not just an asset but a necessity. The effectiveness of a leader's communication can significantly influence the organization's trajectory, impacting everything from team morale to the execution of strategic objectives. Crafting messages that resonate requires a nuanced approach, one that considers the content of the message, the medium through which it is delivered, and the audience it is intended to reach.

Clarity in communication begins with a deep understanding of the message's core. Leaders must distill their ideas into their most essential elements, removing any ambiguity or superfluity that could cloud their message's intent. This clarity of message ensures that every team member, regardless of their role or level of expertise, can grasp the leader's vision and objectives.

To achieve clarity, leaders should employ simple, direct language that conveys their ideas without oversimplification. It involves striking a balance between detail and brevity, providing enough information to foster understanding without overwhelming the audience with unnecessary complexity. Using concrete examples and analogies can also help translate abstract concepts into tangible ideas that are easier for team members to relate to and remember.

22

Beyond clarity, leaders must also master the art of persuasion. Persuasive communication goes beyond merely informing—it motivates and inspires action. It connects the leader's vision and goals with the values, needs, and aspirations of their team members, making the message not just understood but also personally relevant and compelling.

Persuasion in leadership communication often involves:

- **Emphasizing the Why**: Explaining the rationale behind decisions and visions helps team members understand the broader context and the importance of their contributions.
- **Appealing to Shared Values**: Linking the message to the organization's core values can galvanize teams by appealing to a collective sense of purpose and identity.
- **Highlighting Benefits and Addressing Concerns**: Clearly outlining the benefits of a proposed action or change, while also acknowledging and addressing potential concerns, can help mitigate resistance and foster buy-in.

An essential aspect of crafting messages that resonate is the customization of the communication to suit the audience. Leaders must be adept at adjusting their messaging based on the diverse needs, preferences, and cultural backgrounds of their team members. This tailoring involves not only the content of the message but also the tone, style, and delivery method.

23

Understanding the audience entails considering factors such as their level of knowledge about the subject, their interests, and how they are likely to be impacted by the message. For instance, technical details that are crucial for a development team might be less relevant for a marketing team. Similarly, a message that inspires one part of the organization might not resonate with another due to cultural or departmental differences.

In today's digital age, leaders have access to a myriad of communication channels, each with its advantages and contexts of use. From traditional meetings and written memos to emails, social media, and collaboration platforms, the choice of channel can significantly affect the message's reception.

Leaders should select the most appropriate channel based on the message's nature, urgency, and the audience's preferences. For instance, complex or sensitive information might be best communicated through face-to-face meetings where immediate feedback can be obtained, while updates and acknowledgments might be effectively conveyed through email or team messaging apps. Employing a mix of channels can also ensure that the message reaches the audience in multiple forms, reinforcing its impact.

Crafting clear messages is not a one-way street; it requires active engagement with the audience. Leaders must cultivate a culture of active listening, where feedback is sought and valued. This engagement

24

allows leaders to gauge the effectiveness of their communication, understand the perspectives and concerns of their team members, and adjust their messages accordingly.

Feedback mechanisms can take various forms, from direct conversations and surveys to suggestion boxes and interactive Q&A sessions. These channels not only provide insights into how the message is received but also demonstrate the leader's commitment to transparency and dialogue, further enhancing the message's resonance.

Leaders should view each communication as an opportunity to learn and refine their approach. By reflecting on what worked well and what did not, leaders can develop a more intuitive sense of how to communicate effectively with their teams.

This commitment to improvement might involve seeking out training and resources on communication skills, experimenting with different message framings and delivery channels, and soliciting regular feedback from team members and peers. Over time, leaders can develop a communication style that is not only clear and persuasive but also authentically their own, enhancing their ability to inspire and lead their teams toward shared goals and visions.

Crafting messages that resonate is a critical skill in the leader's toolkit, essential for translating vision into action and fostering an environment of mutual understanding and commitment. By focusing on clarity, persuasion, audience customization, and the strategic use of communication channels, leaders can ensure that their messages not only reach their intended audience but also motivate and inspire. Coupled with active listening and a commitment to continuous improvement, these strategies can significantly enhance the effectiveness of leadership communication, paving the way for organizational success.

Open Dialogue

In the landscape of effective leadership, the cultivation of open dialogue stands as a pivotal practice, essential not just for the seamless flow of information but as a cornerstone for building trust, fostering innovation, and enhancing team cohesion. This multifaceted approach to communication emphasizes not only the leader's ability to convey messages but equally prioritizes listening, feedback integration, and adaptability. Through exploring the nuances of open dialogue, we aim to delineate how these practices not only bolster team dynamics but also significantly uplift an organization's problem-solving capabilities and overall productivity.

Open dialogue establishes an environment where ideas flow freely, and feedback is not just encouraged but is seen as a vital

26

component of growth and improvement. It is a two-way street where the leader actively listens and responds to the team's input, fostering a culture of mutual respect and shared responsibility. This form of communication is instrumental in breaking down hierarchical barriers, making it easier for team members to contribute their perspectives, concerns, and innovative ideas without fear of reprisal or dismissal.

One of the foundational benefits of open dialogue is the cultivation of trust within the team. When leaders engage in transparent communication, openly sharing information about decisions, challenges, and the organization's direction, it creates a sense of security and inclusion among team members. Trust is further reinforced when leaders demonstrate vulnerability, admitting to mistakes and showing genuine interest in their team's opinions and wellbeing. This level of honesty not only humanizes the leader but also encourages a similar openness among team members, creating a strong foundation for collaborative problem-solving.

Open dialogue is a powerful tool for enhancing team cohesion. By facilitating regular and open exchanges, team members develop a deeper understanding of each other's strengths, weaknesses, and working styles. This understanding is crucial for fostering a sense of unity and shared purpose. Furthermore, when team members feel their voices are heard and valued, it bolsters their sense of belonging and commitment to the team's objectives. The collaborative atmosphere

27

nurtured by open dialogue ensures that the team moves forward cohesively, leveraging diverse perspectives for innovative solutions.

Integral to the concept of open dialogue are the feedback mechanisms that facilitate the continuous exchange of information between leaders and their teams. These mechanisms can range from structured processes like regular performance reviews and feedback sessions to more informal channels such as open-door policies and suggestion boxes. The key is to ensure that feedback is not just a one-off event but a continuous loop that informs decision-making and process improvements.

For feedback to be effective, it must be constructive and delivered in a manner that fosters growth and development. Leaders play a crucial role in setting the tone for how feedback is given and received within the team. By modeling constructive feedback— highlighting positives as well as areas for improvement—leaders can create an environment where feedback is viewed as a tool for learning rather than criticism. Training sessions on effective feedback techniques can further enhance this skill across the team, ensuring that feedback contributes positively to individual and team development.

Feedback serves as a critical input for adaptability, allowing leaders and teams to pivot their strategies in response to changing circumstances or new information. By actively soliciting and integrating feedback, leaders can make informed decisions that reflect the

28

collective insights of their team. This adaptability is crucial for navigating complex challenges and seizing opportunities for innovation. Moreover, when team members see their feedback leading to tangible changes, it reinforces their sense of agency and investment in the team's success.

Open dialogue, underpinned by effective feedback mechanisms, significantly enhances an organization's problem-solving capabilities. By fostering an environment where diverse viewpoints are sought and valued, leaders can tap into a wider pool of ideas and solutions. This diversity of thought is essential for creative problem-solving, helping teams to identify and address potential blind spots in their strategies.

The practice of open dialogue effectively releases the collective intelligence of the team. When team members from different backgrounds and areas of expertise come together to share their perspectives, the result is a more comprehensive analysis of issues and a richer set of potential solutions. This collaborative approach not only leads to more effective problem-solving but also accelerates the innovation process, as ideas are iteratively refined and improved upon through open discussion.

In today's fast-paced and ever-changing business environment, the ability to respond swiftly and effectively to challenges is a key determinant of success. Open dialogue plays a critical role in facilitating this agility, enabling teams to quickly surface issues, brainstorm solutions, and implement changes. By maintaining open channels of communication, leaders can ensure that their teams are able to adapt rapidly, turning potential obstacles into opportunities for growth and learning.

In essence, fostering open dialogue within the leadership context is about creating a culture of transparency, trust, and collaboration. It involves not only speaking and disseminating information but actively listening, valuing feedback, and being willing to adapt based on collective insights. Through the practices of open dialogue, leaders can strengthen team cohesion, enhance problem-solving capabilities, and lead their organizations toward sustained success. The journey towards mastering open dialogue is continuous, requiring leaders to remain committed to personal growth and to cultivating an environment where every voice is heard, and every perspective is valued.

Summary

Effective communication transcends the mere exchange of information to emerge as a foundational attribute of impactful leadership. It is the golden thread that weaves through the fabric of leadership, binding together the vision of the future with the realities of the present. In a world inundated with information, the clarity of message, persuasiveness of purpose, active engagement in listening, and the integration of feedback stand as pillars upon which effective leadership communication is built. These elements, rooted in a bedrock of openness, trust, and mutual respect, form the cornerstone of not just organizational success but also of meaningful connections within the workplace.

The journey of leadership is intrinsically linked to the ability to articulate a vision that resonates, motivates, and inspires. A clear vision acts as a compass, guiding the organization through the tumult of change and uncertainty. However, the power of a vision lies not in its creation but in its communication. It is through the lens of clarity and persuasiveness that a leader's vision can captivate the imagination of their team, transforming abstract ideas into concrete goals that drive forward momentum.

Building trust is another critical aspect of effective communication in leadership. Trust is not given freely; it is earned through consistent, transparent, and open dialogue. It is cultivated in environments where leaders listen more than they speak, where feedback is not only sought but valued and acted upon. This culture of trust lays the groundwork for strong, resilient teams that can withstand the pressures and challenges of the modern business environment.

Moreover, the achievement of organizational goals is inextricably linked to the quality of communication within the

31

leadership framework. Goals are realized when leaders effectively communicate not only the what and the how but also the why. It is this understanding and alignment of purpose that galvanizes teams to action, fostering collaboration and innovation. Active listening and feedback integration are critical in this process, ensuring that communication is a two-way street and that the path toward these goals adapts and evolves in response to new information and perspectives.

Differences in perception, cultural barriers, and the ever-present risk of misinterpretation can all hinder the communication process. However, these challenges only serve to underscore the importance of striving for excellence in communication. Leaders must be vigilant in their efforts to refine and enhance their communication skills, recognizing that the essence of leadership lies in the ability to connect with people on a deep and meaningful level.

Effective communication is not just a tool of leadership; it is the heart and soul of effective leadership. It is through communication that visions are shared, trust is built, and goals are achieved. The art of communication, therefore, is not merely a skill to be developed but a commitment to understanding, engaging with, and valuing the people who make up an organization. As leaders navigate the complexities of the modern business landscape, let them remember that at the heart of every successful endeavor lies the power of connection, and at the core of connection lies the art of communication.

3.Integrity

Integrity, the third cornerstone of true leadership, extends beyond the mere adherence to ethical guidelines; it embodies the congruence of words and actions that engenders an atmosphere of trust and respect within an organization. It is the silent yet powerful force that shapes the ethical backbone of effective leadership, guiding both the leader's personal conduct and the organization's ethical compass. In our leadership journey, we must explore the multifaceted role of integrity in leadership, underscoring its significance in cultivating a culture where honesty, accountability, and loyalty are not just expected but are ingrained in the very fabric of the organizational identity.

At its core, integrity in leadership is about being truthful and consistent in all actions, decisions, and communications. It means that a leader's public statements align with their private actions, and they fulfill their promises with unwavering commitment. This consistency builds a foundation of trust that is critical for effective leadership. Followers are more likely to believe in the vision and directives of a leader who acts with integrity, seeing them as credible and trustworthy. Moreover, integrity acts as a moral compass during challenging times, guiding leaders to make decisions that uphold the organization's values and ethical standards.

33

The influence of a leader's integrity has a dynamic impact on their team. Leaders who demonstrate integrity create an environment where team members feel valued, respected, and understood. This environment fosters open communication, where honesty is valued and mistakes can be acknowledged without fear of retribution. Such transparency encourages a culture of continuous learning and improvement, where accountability is shared, and everyone is committed to achieving collective goals. Moreover, when leaders model integrity, they set a standard for behavior within the team, encouraging team members to act with honesty and respect towards one another, thereby strengthening team cohesion and collaboration.

Integrity also plays a critical role in the decision-making process. Leaders with high integrity are more likely to make decisions that are not only beneficial for the organization in the short term but are also sustainable and ethical in the long run. They weigh the consequences of their decisions on all stakeholders, ensuring that their actions do not compromise the organization's values. This ethical decision-making process enhances the organization's reputation and credibility, which is invaluable in today's business environment where consumers and partners increasingly prioritize ethical considerations in their interactions with organizations.

The cumulative effect of integrity on team dynamics and decision-making significantly contributes to organizational success. A culture of integrity attracts and retains talent, as employees are more likely to stay with an organization that aligns with their personal values. It also builds trust with customers, suppliers, and partners, laying the foundation for lasting relationships that contribute to sustained success. Furthermore, organizations led by individuals with high integrity are better positioned to navigate ethical dilemmas and crises, emerging with their reputations intact and often strengthened.

Integrity is essential for building trust, fostering a positive organizational culture, making ethical decisions, and ultimately achieving organizational success. It is the steadfast adherence to a set of ethical principles that not only guides a leader's personal actions but also shapes the ethical standards of the organization they lead. By demonstrating integrity, leaders not only earn the trust and respect of their followers but also set a powerful example that promotes a culture of honesty, accountability, and loyalty throughout the organization. As we delve deeper into the importance of integrity in leadership, it becomes clear that its impact extends far beyond the individual, influencing team dynamics, decision-making processes, and the overall success of the organization.

Building Trust

In the complex tapestry of leadership, integrity stands as a fundamental thread, weaving through the very essence of what it means to lead with honor, trust, and ethical clarity. It's about embodying ethical behavior in every action, every decision, and every interaction, thereby ensuring that the team's and organization's best interests are always at the forefront. Acting with integrity serves as a cornerstone for building and maintaining trust, guiding ethical behavior, and fostering decision-making processes that prioritize the collective good.

Trust, the bedrock of any meaningful relationship, is particularly paramount in the leader-follower dynamic. It's cultivated over time, through consistent and reliable actions that align with spoken commitments. Leaders who personify integrity understand that trust is not automatically granted; it is earned through demonstrable actions that reflect an unwavering commitment to their values. This alignment between words and deeds serves as a powerful testament to their character, reassuring team members that their leader is not only dependable but also deeply committed to upholding the principles of honesty, fairness, and ethical conduct.

Ethical behavior is the outward manifestation of a leader's internal value system. It involves making choices that are not only legally compliant but also morally sound, even when faced with situations

36

where unethical conduct might offer the path of least resistance. Leaders with high integrity navigate these challenges by adhering to a moral compass that consistently points towards doing what is right, not just what is expedient. This commitment to ethical behavior serves as a model for the entire organization, setting a standard that influences the organizational culture and guides the conduct of every team member.

Making decisions that reflect the best interests of both the team and the organization at large entails a leadership approach that considers the well-being and development of team members, the sustainability of the organization, and the impact on the broader community and environment. Such decision-making processes are often characterized by transparency, inclusiveness, and a balanced consideration of short-term challenges and long-term objectives. By prioritizing the collective good in decision-making, leaders not only exemplify ethical leadership but also foster a sense of shared purpose and mutual respect within their teams.

The process of building trust through integrity is continuous and dynamic. It requires leaders to consistently demonstrate their commitment to their values, even under pressure or in the face of adversity. Maintaining trust necessitates a proactive approach to communication, ensuring that team members are informed, engaged, and feel valued in the decision-making process. It also involves acknowledging mistakes and taking responsibility for them—a powerful demonstration of integrity that reinforces trust by showing that the leader is accountable and committed to learning and improvement.

Leaders are often faced with situations that test their integrity, from ethical dilemmas to conflicts of interest. Navigating these challenges with integrity involves a thoughtful analysis of the ethical implications of various options, seeking counsel from trusted advisors, and making decisions that can be openly justified based on ethical principles. This approach not only strengthens the leader's moral authority but also instills confidence in team members that their leader is guided by a strong ethical framework.

The influence of a leader's integrity extends beyond individual relationships to shape the entire organizational culture. A culture rooted in integrity is one where ethical conduct is the norm, transparency is valued, and accountability is embedded in all processes. In such an environment, team members feel empowered to speak up, share their ideas and concerns, and contribute to a culture of continuous improvement. This positive organizational culture, in turn, enhances team cohesion, boosts morale, and attracts talent who share the organization's commitment to ethical excellence.

Leaders who embody integrity pave the way for organizational success by fostering a work environment where trust flourishes, ethical behavior is celebrated, and decisions are made with the collective best interests in mind. This environment encourages innovation, facilitates

38

effective problem-solving, and enhances adaptability, enabling the organization to navigate the complexities of the modern business landscape with agility and resilience. Ultimately, integrity in leadership not only contributes to the achievement of organizational goals but also builds a lasting legacy of ethical excellence and meaningful impact.

Integrity is not just a desirable attribute but an essential one. It underpins the ability to build and maintain trust, guides ethical behavior, and informs decision-making processes that prioritize the collective good. By aligning their actions with their values and commitments, leaders can foster a culture of honesty, accountability, and loyalty that propels both individuals and the organization towards unparalleled heights of achievement. The pursuit of integrity in leadership is a journey marked by continuous reflection, steadfast commitment, and an unwavering dedication to doing what is right. It is a journey well worth undertaking, for at the end lies not just organizational success, but a legacy of positive impact that transcends the boundaries of the organization itself.

Organizational Contributions

The essence of integrity in leadership can have a significant and lasting impact on an organization's reputation, both internally among

39

employees and externally among customers, partners, and the broader community. This deep-rooted value influences every facet of organizational life, from attracting top talent to ensuring sustainability and longevity. By dissecting the role of integrity in shaping an organization's reputation, we uncover the profound influence ethical leadership has on fostering a reputable and sustainable organization.

Leaders who consistently demonstrate honesty, transparency, and ethical decision-making earn the respect and trust of their employees. This internal reputation is crucial for creating an environment where team members feel valued, understood, and motivated. Employees are more likely to commit to a leader's vision and directives when they believe in the leader's integrity. This trust fosters a culture of open communication, where feedback is encouraged and challenges can be addressed collaboratively. Moreover, leaders who practice what they preach, acknowledging their mistakes and being accountable for their actions, reinforce a culture of integrity that permeates the entire organization.

Externally, the integrity of organizational leadership plays a pivotal role in shaping the public's perception. In an era where consumers are increasingly concerned with corporate ethics, organizations led by principled leaders are often viewed more favorably. This positive external reputation can enhance customer loyalty, attract business partnerships, and elevate the organization's standing within the community and industry. Ethical leadership practices, such as fair

40

dealing, commitment to social responsibilities, and transparency in operations, signal to external stakeholders that the organization is trustworthy and reliable. Over time, this reputation for integrity can become one of the organization's most valuable assets, differentiating it in a competitive marketplace and providing a foundation for enduring success.

An organization's reputation for integrity serves as a powerful magnet for attracting high-quality talent. Prospective employees are drawn to environments where ethical conduct is valued and where they can align their personal values with their professional endeavors. This alignment is increasingly important to the modern workforce, who seek purpose and fulfillment in their roles. Organizations known for their ethical leadership practices and commitment to integrity are likely to attract individuals who are not only skilled but also highly motivated and engaged. This influx of like-minded talent further strengthens the organization's culture, enhancing its capabilities and driving innovation.

The integration of integrity within leadership is intrinsically linked to sustainable practices and the long-term success of the organization. Leaders who prioritize ethical considerations in their decision-making processes are more likely to adopt strategies that are not just profitable but also sustainable. This approach considers the welfare of employees, the community, and the environment, leading to decisions that support long-term organizational success. Such practices not only mitigate risks and reduce potential legal and financial liabilities

41

but also appeal to a broader stakeholder base, including environmentally and socially conscious consumers and investors. Consequently, integrity in leadership fosters a business model that is resilient, adaptable, and geared towards longevity.

The role of integrity in building a strong reputation, both internally and externally, is a critical component of effective leadership, influencing trust and follower-ship within the organization, shaping the public's perception, attracting top talent, and ensuring sustainable and long-term success. Leaders who embody integrity lay the groundwork for a reputable and resilient organization, capable of navigating the complexities of the modern business environment while maintaining its ethical compass. As such, integrity should be nurtured and prioritized at all levels of leadership, serving as a guiding principle for decision-making, operations, and the overall strategic direction of the organization. In doing so, organizations can achieve not only success but also significance in their contributions to society and the broader business landscape.

Summary

Integrity is a fundamental virtue in the pantheon of leadership qualities seen in effective leaders. It's not just a matter of following the rules or adhering to guidelines; it's about aligning one's actions with their words, a harmony that becomes the bedrock of trust and respect in any organization. This congruence between what leaders say and do acts as the ethical backbone of leadership, influencing not just their personal conduct but also setting the moral compass for the entire organization. As we delve deeper into the essence of integrity in leadership, we uncover its pivotal role in sculpting an organizational culture steeped in honesty, accountability, and unwavering loyalty.

Integrity in leadership is the silent guardian of an organization's ethical standing. It is the invisible force that guides leaders to act not just for the immediate gains but for the long-term welfare of their teams and the organization at large. This commitment to ethical behavior and decisions that mirror one's spoken words fosters a deep sense of trust among team members. Trust, in this context, becomes more than a mere expectation; it transforms into a tangible experience, palpable in the daily interactions and operational ethos of the organization. The trust cultivated through integrity encourages openness, where ideas are shared freely, and innovation thrives.

Moreover, integrity serves as the cornerstone for cultivating a culture of accountability. In an environment where leaders exemplify integrity, accountability becomes a shared value, a collective commitment rather than an imposed obligation. It creates a workspace where mistakes are acknowledged as part of the learning process, and taking responsibility is viewed as a strength. This culture of

43

accountability, underpinned by integrity, ensures that every member of the organization feels responsible not just for their successes but also for their failures, viewing them as opportunities for growth and improvement.

Loyalty, too, finds its roots in the fertile ground of integrity. When leaders consistently demonstrate integrity, they engender a deep sense of loyalty among their followers. This loyalty is born out of respect and admiration for leaders who stand by their principles, even when faced with adversity. It's a loyalty that transcends the transactional nature of work, fostering a sense of belonging and commitment to the organization's vision and goals. In such an environment, loyalty becomes a two-way street, with leaders and team members mutually committed to each other's success and the success of the organization.

The role of integrity in leadership cannot be is the potent force that molds the ethical landscape of an organization, guiding it through the challenges of the modern business world. As leaders, the journey towards embodying integrity involves a continuous commitment to aligning our actions with our words, fostering an atmosphere of trust, accountability, and loyalty. By prioritizing integrity, we can cultivate an organizational culture that not only expects but embodies these values, ensuring the long-term success and ethical standing of our organizations. In the realm of leadership, integrity is not just a virtue to be admired but a principle to live by, integral to the very identity of effective, transformative leadership.

4.Empathy

Empathy allows leaders to connect with their team members on a deeper level, fostering a supportive and inclusive environment. The role of empathy in leadership, at its core, is about understanding and caring about the well-being of team members can lead to enhanced motivation, performance, and loyalty. It fosters a culture where emotional intelligence guides interactions and decisions. This capability enables leaders to forge deep connections with their team members, creating a work environment that is not only supportive and inclusive but also conducive to heightened motivation, performance, and loyalty.

Empathetic leadership is about seeing the world through the eyes of your team members and understanding their challenges, aspirations, and concerns without judgment. It involves active listening, where the leader is fully present, giving their undivided attention to understand the underlying messages conveyed by their team members. This form of leadership acknowledges the personal and professional lives of team members as interconnected realms, understanding that support in one area invariably benefits the other.

Empathy plays a crucial role in cultivating an environment where every individual feels valued and understood. By demonstrating empathy, leaders send a powerful message that the organization cares about its employees beyond their professional contributions. This approach encourages a culture of openness, where team members feel comfortable sharing their ideas and challenges, knowing they will be met with understanding and support. In such an environment, diversity is celebrated, and inclusivity is practiced, leading to a richer, more creative, and collaborative workplace.

When leaders show genuine concern for the well-being of their team members, it fosters a sense of belonging and significance among employees. This emotional investment creates a motivational boost, as team members feel their work is meaningful and recognized. Moreover, empathetic leaders are adept at identifying the unique motivators of each team member, allowing them to tailor their approach to inspire high performance. This personalized motivation strategy ensures that team members are engaged, challenged, and satisfied with their work, leading to higher productivity and quality of output.

Loyalty, a coveted trait in the organizational context, is significantly influenced by the presence of empathy. Team members are more likely to develop a strong allegiance to a leader and an organization that demonstrates care for their personal and professional growth. This loyalty is not born out of obligation but from a deep-seated appreciation for the empathetic support provided by the leadership. In times of organizational change or external challenges, this loyalty translates into resilience and commitment, as team members are more willing to stand by their leaders and the organization.

Implementing empathetic leadership requires intentional practice and reflection. Leaders can enhance their empathy skills through various means:

- **Active Listening**: Dedicate time for open conversations with team members, encouraging them to share their thoughts and feelings.
- **Empathy Training**: Engage in training programs designed to improve emotional intelligence and empathetic communication.
- **Feedback Mechanisms**: Establish systems that allow for anonymous feedback on leadership practices, ensuring that employees feel safe to express their concerns.
- **Supportive Policies**: Develop policies that reflect an understanding of team members' needs, such as flexible working hours, mental health days, and professional development opportunities.

Leaders must strive to balance empathy with the ability to make tough decisions that may not always align with the desires of every team member. Moreover, leaders must guard against empathy fatigue, where the emotional toll of connecting deeply with many individuals can become overwhelming. Setting boundaries and practicing self-care are essential for leaders to maintain their emotional well-being and continue to offer effective, empathetic leadership.

The Power Of Empathy

Empathetic leadership, characterized by a leader's ability to understand can be a transformative approach in today's organizational dynamics. Transcending traditional leadership models by prioritizing emotional intelligence and fostering deeper human connections, the benefits of such leadership are expansive. Exercising empathy can have profound impacts not only the interpersonal relationships within the team but also enhances communication and cultivates a nurturing organizational culture.

The ability to forge strong, meaningful relationships with team members lies at the heart of empathetic leadership. Empathy allows leaders to step into the shoes of their employees, understanding their personal and professional challenges with a depth that exceeds superficial engagement. This understanding fosters a sense of mutual respect and trust, forming the bedrock of strong relationships. When team members feel genuinely cared for, not just as employees but as individuals, it creates a bond that enhances teamwork, collaboration, and loyalty. These relationships are characterized by an open exchange

49

of ideas, a willingness to support one another, and a shared commitment to achieving organizational goals.

Empathetic leadership significantly improves communication within the team. By actively listening and responding with sensitivity to the concerns and ideas of team members, leaders can create an environment where open, honest dialogue is encouraged. Empathy involves not only understanding what is being said but also recognizing the emotions and unspoken thoughts behind the words. This level of communication goes beyond the transactional to build a foundation of trust and openness. Improved communication leads to clearer understanding of tasks, more effective collaboration, and the ability to address and resolve conflicts constructively.

One of the most significant benefits of empathetic leadership is its ability to cultivate a supportive and inclusive organizational culture. In a culture where empathy is valued, team members feel acknowledged and appreciated, boosting their sense of belonging and self-worth. This type of culture encourages individuals to express themselves freely, share their unique perspectives, and contribute fully to the team's efforts. It also promotes diversity and inclusion, as empathy involves valuing and seeking to understand the broad range of experiences and backgrounds that team members bring to the table. In such an environment, innovation flourishes, as people feel safe to take risks, experiment with new ideas, and learn from their failures without fear of judgment or retribution.

50

Empathetic leadership empowers team members by acknowledging their strengths, encouraging their growth, and providing support for their challenges. Leaders who show empathy are better equipped to recognize the potential in their team members, tailor opportunities for their development, and provide constructive feedback that motivates improvement. This empowerment leads to increased self-efficacy among team members, as they feel their contributions are valued and they have the support needed to excel. Empowered employees are more engaged, motivated, and committed to the organization's success, driving higher levels of performance and productivity.

The emotional well-being of employees has become increasingly important in today's high-stress work environments. Empathetic leadership plays a crucial role in nurturing this well-being by creating a supportive atmosphere where the emotional needs of team members are recognized and addressed. Leaders who practice empathy demonstrate understanding and compassion for the personal challenges that team members may face, whether related to work or their personal lives. This compassionate approach can reduce stress, prevent burnout, and contribute to a healthier work-life balance for employees. Furthermore, by prioritizing the emotional well-being of their team, empathetic leaders contribute to a more positive, energized, and resilient workforce.

By building strong relationships, enhancing communication, fostering a supportive culture, empowering team members, and

51

nurturing emotional well-being, empathetic leaders can create an environment where individuals feel valued, understood, and motivated to contribute their best. The ripple effects of such leadership extend beyond individual team members, influencing the overall health, performance, and success of the organization. As businesses continue to navigate the complexities of the modern workplace, empathy has emerged as a critical ingredient for creating a thriving, resilient, and inclusive organizational culture.

Practical Strategies

Developing and demonstrating empathy as a leader is pivotal in creating an environment where team members feel genuinely supported and understood. This supportive atmosphere not only enhances individual and team performance but also fosters a culture of trust, inclusivity, and collaboration. There are several practical strategies for leaders aiming to cultivate empathy in their leadership style:

Active Listening: Active listening is the cornerstone of empathetic leadership. It involves fully concentrating on what is being said rather than just passively hearing the message. Leaders can practice active listening by:

- **Giving Full Attention**: Eliminate distractions and focus entirely on the speaker. Non-verbal cues, such as eye contact and nodding, signal that you are engaged and attentive.
- **Reflecting and Clarifying**: Paraphrase or summarize what you've heard to confirm understanding. Ask clarifying questions to delve deeper into the speaker's perspective.
- **Withholding Judgment**: Approach each conversation with an open mind, avoiding premature judgment or offering unsolicited advice.
- **Demonstrating Understanding**: Use empathetic statements to show you understand the speaker's feelings and viewpoints.

Acknowledging Emotions: Recognizing and validating the emotions of team members is a powerful way to demonstrate empathy. Leaders can:

- **Name the Emotion**: Sometimes, simply identifying and naming the emotion a team member is experiencing can validate their feelings and make them feel understood.
- **Express Understanding**: Use phrases like "It sounds like you're feeling..." to show that you're trying to understand their emotional state.
- **Avoid Minimizing**: Resist the urge to dismiss or minimize their feelings, even if the solution seems straightforward. Acknowledgment doesn't always require agreement but understanding.

53

Supporting Growth And Development: Empathy extends to supporting the professional growth and personal development of team members. Leaders can:

- **Identify Individual Aspirations**: Spend time understanding the personal goals and aspirations of each team member. This knowledge allows for more personalized support and development opportunities.
- **Provide Meaningful Opportunities**: Offer assignments that challenge your team members in areas they are passionate about or wish to develop. This shows trust in their abilities and commitment to their growth.
- **Offer Constructive Feedback**: Feedback should be aimed at development, focusing on specific behaviors or outcomes and suggesting actionable steps for improvement. Ensure that feedback sessions are two-way conversations where team members can express their thoughts and feelings.
- **Celebrate Successes**: Recognize and celebrate achievements, both big and small. Public acknowledgment can boost morale and motivation, while also demonstrating your attention to their efforts and progress.

Cultivate A Culture Of Empathy: Beyond individual actions, leaders can foster an organizational culture where empathy is valued and practiced by all. This involves:

- **Modeling Empathetic Behavior**: Be the example. The way you interact with team members sets the tone for how they treat each other.
- **Training and Resources**: Provide training sessions or workshops focused on developing emotional intelligence and empathy skills across the organization.
- **Creating Safe Spaces**: Establish forums or regular meetings where team members can share their thoughts, feelings, and challenges without fear of judgment or repercussions.
- **Encouraging Peer Support**: Promote a culture of peer mentoring and support, where team members can turn to each other for advice, feedback, and encouragement.

For leaders aiming to enhance their empathetic leadership, the journey involves a continuous commitment to understanding and supporting their team members' emotional and professional needs. By practicing active listening, acknowledging emotions, and fostering growth and development, leaders can build a strong foundation of trust and loyalty. Moreover, by embedding empathy into the organizational culture, leaders can create an environment where team members feel valued, understood, and motivated to achieve their best, driving the organization toward greater success and fulfillment.

Summary

Developing and demonstrating empathy is not merely a beneficial trait; it is a leadership imperative, fostering an environment where team members feel deeply supported and comprehensively understood. The implications of such empathetic leadership extend far beyond the confines of individual interactions, permeating the very fiber of the organization's culture and ethos. This supportive atmosphere catalyzes a remarkable enhancement in both individual and team performance, establishing a foundation built on trust, inclusivity, and collaboration. It cultivates a workspace where diversity of thought is not only encouraged but celebrated, and where the emotional and professional well-being of every team member is prioritized.

Honing your empathetic leadership skills requires a conscious, deliberate effort to integrate empathy into daily leadership practices. Practically, this begins with active listening, a skill that demands full engagement and presence, enabling leaders to understand the underlying messages and emotions conveyed by their team members. Such depth of understanding forms the basis for meaningful connections, fostering a sense of belonging and validation among team members. By acknowledging and validating the emotions and perspectives of others leaders can dismantle barriers to open communication.

56

The role of empathy is integral in supporting the growth and development of team members. By identifying and aligning with the individual aspirations and needs of each team member, leaders can tailor opportunities for professional development and personal growth. This personalized support not only boosts morale and motivation but also drives performance and productivity. Constructive feedback, framed within an empathetic understanding, serves as a powerful tool for development, motivating team members to strive for excellence while feeling supported and valued.

Empathetic leadership is evidenced by an organizational culture that mirrors these values. Creating safe spaces for open dialogue, promoting peer support, and modeling empathetic behavior are pivotal strategies that underscore the importance of emotional intelligence within the workplace. Such an environment nurtures resilience, encourages innovation, and enhances adaptability, equipping the organization to navigate the complexities of the modern business landscape with agility and strength.

Furthermore, the benefits of empathetic leadership resonate beyond the immediate team environment, influencing the organization's external reputation. In today's socially connected world, the values and culture of an organization are more visible than ever. A leadership style characterized by empathy and inclusivity attracts talent, strengthens customer relations, and builds lasting partnerships. It signals potential

57

customers, investors, and employees that the organization is committed to ethical practices and values the human element of business.

The role of empathy in leadership is indispensable in shaping an organizational culture that values, supports, and understands its team members. By embracing empathy, leaders can forge deeper connections, enhance performance, and build a resilient, inclusive culture that leads to success. This approach not only achieves superior results but also contributes to a legacy of leadership that is both impactful and enduring.

5.Decisiveness

In the complex and fast-paced world of leadership, the capacity to make timely and informed decisions stands as a hallmark of effective leadership. This pivotal skill differentiates leaders who are merely competent from those who are truly transformative, enabling them to guide their teams through challenges and opportunities with precision and insight. Decisiveness is of critical importance and leaders must strike a delicate balance between conducting thorough analysis and acting with the necessary urgency.

Decisiveness is not just about the speed of making decisions but also about the quality and impact of these decisions on the team and the organization. It involves a nuanced understanding of the situation at hand, the ability to sift through those data and opinions to identify the most relevant information, and the courage to take a stand, even in the face of ambiguity and uncertainty.

At the core of decisive leadership lies the ability to make tough decisions—a process fraught with challenges but rich with potential for significant positive impact. Leaders should endeavor for deep understanding of the decision-making process, emphasizing the importance of aligning decisions with the organization's overarching vision and values. Leaders often encounter situations where the information available is incomplete, and the outcomes of their decisions are uncertain. Navigating this complexity requires a robust framework for evaluating options and considering the broader implications of each potential choice.

Luckily, there are strategies for systematic analysis and critical thinking that enable leaders to dissect complex problems, weigh the pros and cons of different courses of action, and anticipate the potential consequences of their decisions. As leaders seeking to improve these skills, we must develop tactics for overcoming biases, dealing with the pressure of high-stakes situations, and maintaining a clear focus on long-term objectives over short-term gains.

Change is an inevitable part of the business landscape, often bringing with it a degree of uncertainty and disruption. In these moments, the ability of leaders to make decisive, confident decisions becomes even more critical. Leaders must have the aptitude for clarity and confidence in decision-making during times of change or crisis.

Decision-Making Strategies

Practical decision-making strategies are essential tools for leaders who face the daunting task of making difficult decisions amidst

60

uncertainty and complexity. These strategies provide a structured approach to navigate the challenges inherent in the decision-making process, enabling leaders to make informed choices that align with their organization's vision and values. Below are key strategies and considerations for leaders to enhance their decision-making capabilities.

Establish a Clear Decision-Making Framework: A structured framework serves as a guide through the decision-making process, ensuring consistency and thoroughness. This might include:

- **Defining the Problem**: Clearly articulate what needs to be solved, ensuring understanding across the team.
- **Identifying Objectives**: Determine what the decision aims to achieve, aligning with the organization's goals.
- **Gathering Information**: Collect relevant data and insights, recognizing when there's enough information to proceed despite uncertainties.
- **Generating Options**: Encourage diverse thinking to produce multiple potential solutions, fostering creativity and innovation.

Align Decisions with Vision and Values: Decisions should not only address immediate concerns but also contribute to the long-term mission and ethos of the organization. Leaders should:

- **Reflect on Core Values**: Ensure that each option is evaluated against the organization's core values, choosing paths that reinforce these principles.
- **Consider Long-term Impact**: Evaluate how each decision aligns with the long-term vision, prioritizing choices that propel the organization towards its overarching goals.

Embrace a Collaborative Approach: Involving key stakeholders in the decision-making process can provide new perspectives, enhance buy-in, and mitigate resistance. Leaders should:

- **Seek Diverse Perspectives**: Consult team members, peers, and external advisors to broaden the understanding of the issue and potential solutions.
- **Foster an Inclusive Environment**: Create a safe space for open dialogue where all opinions are valued, encouraging constructive debate and collaboration.

Evaluate Options with a Critical Eye: Analyzing the potential outcomes and implications of each option is crucial for making informed decisions. Leaders should:

62

- **Conduct a SWOT Analysis**: Assess the Strengths, Weaknesses, Opportunities, and Threats associated with each option.
- **Consider the Worst-case Scenario**: Understanding the potential risks and developing contingency plans can prepare the organization for adverse outcomes.

Communicate Decisions with Confidence: Once a decision is made, leaders should communicate it clearly and confidently to their team, explaining the rationale and expected outcomes. This includes:

- **Communicating Effectively**: Share the decision-making process and reasoning behind the choice, ensuring transparency and understanding.
- **Building Trust through Transparency**: Demonstrate how the decision aligns with the organization's values and vision, reinforcing trust in leadership.

Learn from Outcomes: Every decision, whether successful or not, offers valuable lessons. Leaders should:

- **Review and Reflect**: Analyze the outcomes of decisions to understand what worked, what didn't, and why.

63

- **Foster a Learning Culture**: Encourage the team to view mistakes as learning opportunities, continuously improving decision-making processes.

Analytic Strategies

Systematic analysis and critical thinking are indispensable tools in a leader's arsenal, enabling them to navigate the intricacies of complex decision-making with precision and foresight. These strategies not only aid in dissecting complex problems but also in evaluating the various courses of action and their potential outcomes. Below, we delve into specific strategies, complemented by examples, to illustrate how leaders can apply systematic analysis and critical thinking in their decision-making processes.

SWOT Analysis involves examining the Strengths, Weaknesses, Opportunities, and Threats related to a particular decision or problem. This comprehensive approach allows leaders to assess internal and external factors that could impact their decision.

Example: *A tech company considering the launch of a new product might use a SWOT analysis to assess its internal capabilities*

(Strengths: innovative technology, skilled team; Weaknesses: limited marketing budget) and external factors (Opportunities: emerging market demand; Threats: strong competition). This analysis helps the company's leadership understand whether they should proceed with the launch, delay it until they can secure more funding for marketing, or refine the product to better compete in the market.

Cost-Benefit Analysis is a quantitative approach to comparing the costs and benefits of different decisions. It helps leaders to quantify outcomes and make choices that offer the greatest benefit relative to cost.

Example: A healthcare organization considering the adoption of a new electronic health records system might perform a cost-benefit analysis. This would involve calculating the costs of purchasing and implementing the new system (training staff, data migration, software costs) against the benefits (improved patient care, efficiency gains, reduced paperwork). The leadership decides to adopt the new system as the long-term benefits significantly outweigh the initial costs.

Scenario Planning involves imagining various future scenarios that could result from a decision and planning for those possibilities. It helps leaders anticipate changes and adapt their strategies accordingly.

65

Example: A retail chain faced with declining sales might use scenario planning to consider different futures, such as the impact of doubling down on e-commerce, closing underperforming stores, or pivoting to luxury products. For each scenario, they would assess potential outcomes and develop a strategic response. This foresight enables the company to pivot quickly as market conditions change.

Decision Trees are a visual tool for mapping out the decisions and their possible consequences, including chance event outcomes, resource costs, and utility. It's a way to graphically analyze the various actions and their possible effects.

Example: An investment firm evaluating whether to invest in a startup might use a decision tree to map out the potential outcomes. The tree would include branches for investing or not investing, with further branches representing possible outcomes of each choice (e.g., high return, break even, loss). This visual representation helps the firm's leaders assess the risk and potential reward of the investment.

The Five Whys Technique is a problem-solving method that involves asking "Why?" five times to drill down to the root cause of a problem. It's a simple but effective way to uncover underlying issues that need addressing.

Example: A manufacturing company experiencing a decline in product quality might use the Five Whys to find the root cause. The first why might reveal that machines are malfunctioning more frequently. Asking why again might show that maintenance schedules have been delayed, and further whys could uncover that the maintenance team is understaffed. Recognizing this, leadership decides to hire additional maintenance staff to prevent future quality issues.

By employing these strategies for systematic analysis and critical thinking, leaders can more effectively dissect complex problems, evaluate potential solutions, and anticipate the consequences of their decisions. These examples illustrate the practical application of these strategies across different scenarios, highlighting their versatility and effectiveness in enhancing decision-making processes.

Summary

In the labyrinth of contemporary organizational challenges, the arsenal of a leader must be well-equipped with practical decision-making strategies. These strategies are not just tools for resolving immediate problems but are foundational elements that shape a leader's effectiveness and organizational success. Establishing a clear

67

decision-making framework, ensuring alignment with the organization's core vision and values, fostering an environment of collaboration, engaging in critical evaluation of all possible options, making informed and confident choices, and adopting a learning mindset towards each decision made—these are the pillars upon which decisive leadership stands.

A clear framework for decision-making provides a structured approach that ensures consistency, fairness, and transparency in how decisions are made. This framework is not a rigid set of rules but a flexible guide that adapts to the unique demands of each situation, ensuring that decisions are made with a clear understanding of their implications.

Embracing collaboration in decision-making processes democratizes leadership and taps into the collective wisdom of the team. It encourages diverse perspectives, mitigates biases, and leads to more robust, well-rounded decisions. Collaboration builds a culture of inclusivity, where team members feel valued and invested in the outcomes of their collective efforts.

Critical evaluation of options is what separates reactive decision-making from strategic leadership. It involves a deep dive into the potential benefits and drawbacks of each course of action, considering not just the immediate outcomes but the long-term implications as well.

This critical lens ensures that decisions are not just informed but are made with foresight, anticipating future challenges and opportunities.

Confidence in decision-making stems from a thorough understanding of the issue at hand, a clear evaluation of the options, and an unwavering commitment to the organization's values. This confidence is infectious, inspiring trust and respect among team members and stakeholders alike.

Finally, adopting a learning mindset toward decision-making ensures continuous growth and improvement. Every decision, whether successful or not, is a learning opportunity. Reflecting on the outcomes of decisions, understanding what worked and what didn't, and why, enables leaders to refine their decision-making processes, becoming more adept and effective over time.

This comprehensive approach to decision-making does more than just enhance the effectiveness of leadership. It builds a foundation of trust and loyalty, essential ingredients for fostering a motivated and engaged workforce. Moreover, it sets the organization on a path toward achieving its long-term goals, ensuring sustainability and success in an ever-changing world.

6.Adaptability

In a world characterized by its constant flux and unpredictability, the ability to adapt has become indispensable for leadership. The dynamism of the modern era, marked by rapid technological advancements, shifting market demands, and evolving societal expectations, necessitates leadership skills that are not only reactive but proactively adaptive. Adaptability promotes flexibility and openness. Adaptive leaders are uniquely positioned to anticipate changes, recalibrate strategies accordingly, and shepherd their teams through the myriad transitions and challenges that define our times.

Adaptive leaders are characterized by a distinct set of traits that enable them to thrive in environments of uncertainty and change. Central to this attribute is an openness to change, a quality that allows leaders to view shifts in the landscape not as threats but as opportunities for growth and innovation. Coupled with this openness is resilience, the ability to bounce back from setbacks and failures, using them as stepping stones for future success. Adaptive leaders also possess a remarkable capacity to inspire and guide their teams through uncertainty, instilling a sense of confidence and direction amidst the chaos of change. These traits collectively form the backbone of adaptive leadership and contribute to its effectiveness in steering organizations through uncharted waters.

Leadership today requires actionable strategies for cultivating adaptability within leadership practices. One such strategy involves fostering a culture of innovation, where creativity is encouraged, and new ideas are welcomed. By creating an environment that values innovation, leaders can ensure their organizations remain at the cutting edge, poised to adapt to changes swiftly and effectively.

Encouraging experimentation is another critical strategy for adaptive leadership. Experimentation allows organizations to test new approaches in a controlled, manageable environment, learning from both successes and failures. This practice not only contributes to the organization's adaptability but also reinforces a culture of constant learning and continuous improvement.

Developing flexible plans that can accommodate new information and shifting circumstances is also essential for adaptive leadership. Such plans, often described as 'living documents,' are designed to evolve, incorporating fresh insights and adapting to new realities as they emerge. This approach ensures that organizations can pivot quickly, aligning their strategies with the dynamic environment in which they operate.

Leadership demands more than just a visionary outlook and effective management skills. It necessitates a proactive approach to cultivating adaptability within organizational practices, ensuring that the entity remains resilient and agile in the face of change. A pivotal strategy in achieving this is developing a culture of innovation—a setting where creativity is not just encouraged but is the bedrock of the organization's ethos.

The first step in fostering a culture of innovation is creating an environment that actively values and rewards creative thinking and novel ideas. This involves:

- **Open Communication Channels**: Establishing open lines of communication across all levels of the organization, encouraging employees to share their ideas and feedback without fear of judgment or repercussion.
- **Recognition and Rewards**: Implementing systems to recognize and reward innovative ideas and risk-taking, even when efforts don't always lead to success. This could range from formal awards and incentives to informal acknowledgment in team meetings.
- **Resource Allocation**: Providing the necessary resources, be it time, budget, or tools, for employees to explore new ideas and

conduct experiments. This signals the organization's commitment to innovation and supports the practical pursuit of creative projects.

Encouraging creativity and the generation of new ideas is crucial in maintaining a competitive edge. Leaders can implement:

- **Dedicated Time for Innovation**: Follow the example of companies like Google and 3M by allocating dedicated time for employees to work on projects outside their regular duties, fostering an environment where innovation is part of the job description.
- **Cross-functional Collaboration**: Promote cross-functional teams and projects that bring together diverse perspectives and expertise, enhancing the potential for groundbreaking ideas and solutions.
- **Fostering a Safe-to-Fail Environment**: Cultivate an atmosphere where failure is viewed as a step towards innovation. Encouraging calculated risk-taking and viewing setbacks as learning opportunities are essential in maintaining a dynamic, innovative culture.

The ultimate goal of fostering a culture of innovation is to ensure the organization can adapt to changes swiftly and effectively. This requires:

- **Continuous Learning and Development**: Encouraging continuous learning and development not only in the domain of one's expertise but also in areas related to innovation management and adaptability skills.
- **Leveraging Technology**: Keeping abreast of and leveraging new technologies to enhance operational efficiency, improve product offerings, and streamline communication and collaboration.
- **Strategic Flexibility**: Developing strategic plans that are flexible and can be adjusted as new information comes to light or as circumstances change, ensuring the organization can pivot quickly in response to external pressures.

Leadership today is as much about fostering the right environment as it is about making strategic decisions. By cultivating a culture of innovation, leaders can ensure their organizations are not just surviving but thriving in the modern business landscape. An innovative culture is characterized by a continuous quest for improvement, where creativity and new ideas are the norms, and adaptability is woven into the fabric of the organization's practices. By leaning into innovation,

74

leaders can navigate their teams through the complexities of change, ensuring sustained growth and success in an ever-evolving world.

Encourage Experimentation

Encouraging experimentation within an organization is a pivotal strategy for leaders striving to enhance adaptability and foster a culture of innovation. This approach allows for the testing of new ideas, strategies, and processes in a controlled, manageable environment, thereby minimizing risk while maximizing the potential for discovery and learning. By institutionalizing experimentation, leaders can ensure that their organizations remain agile, responsive to changes, and continuously evolving.

As previously mentioned, adaptive leadership is characterized by a willingness to embrace change and a recognition that the most effective strategies and solutions often emerge from a process of trial and error. Experimentation is central to this approach, providing a structured method for exploring new possibilities, challenging assumptions, and pushing the boundaries of what is currently known or practiced within the organization. A thoughtful leader intent on agility creates an atmosphere where experimentation in a controlled environment is part of the culture.

75

A crucial aspect of encouraging experimentation is the creation of a safe-to-fail environment. This concept acknowledges that not all experiments will lead to success, but every outcome is valuable as a learning opportunity. Leaders play a key role in shaping this environment by:

- **Normalizing Failure**: Communicating that failure is an expected and acceptable part of the experimentation process. This involves celebrating the lessons learned from failed experiments as vigorously as celebrating successes.
- **Setting Clear Parameters**: Defining the scope and boundaries of experiments to ensure that risks are contained and manageable. This clarity helps to mitigate potential negative impacts on the broader organization.

To maximize the benefits of experimentation, organizations can adopt frameworks that guide the design, structure, implementation, and evaluation of experiments. These frameworks often include:

- **Hypothesis-Driven Testing**: Starting each experiment with a clear hypothesis that articulates the expected outcome and the rationale behind it. This approach ensures that experiments are focused and that their results can be meaningfully interpreted.
- **Rapid Prototyping and Iteration**: Developing quick, low-fidelity versions of new products, services, or processes to gather feedback and insights before investing significant resources. This

76

iterative process allows for continuous refinement based on real-world input.

- **Metrics and Measurement**: Establishing clear metrics to evaluate the success of experiments. This could include both quantitative measures, such as performance improvements or cost savings, and qualitative feedback from customers or employees.

The practice of experimentation contributes significantly to the development of a culture that values constant learning and continuous improvement. Leaders can reinforce this culture by:

- **Sharing Learnings Widely**: Ensuring that the insights gained from experiments are disseminated throughout the organization. This could involve formal debriefings, internal case studies, or knowledge-sharing platforms.
- **Encouraging Cross-Functional Collaboration**: Bringing together diverse teams to participate in experimentation efforts. This collaboration can spark new ideas, broaden perspectives, and break down silos within the organization.
- **Rewarding Curiosity and Initiative**: Recognizing and rewarding individuals and teams who propose and participate in experiments. This recognition can take many forms, from public acknowledgment to financial incentives.

77

Encouraging experimentation is a critical strategy for leaders aiming to cultivate adaptability within their organizations. By creating a safe-to-fail environment, leveraging structured experimentation frameworks, and fostering a culture of constant learning and continuous improvement, leaders can ensure that their organizations are well-equipped to navigate the complexities of the modern business landscape. Through experimentation, organizations can unlock new opportunities, drive efficiency, and enhance their competitive edge, all while building a resilient and dynamic organizational culture.

Flexible Planning

Adaptive leadership is heavily dependent on one's ability to be flexible in their planning. These plans, often termed 'living documents,' embody the essence of adaptability, designed to evolve in response to new information, insights, and the inevitable shifts in the external environment. This strategic flexibility allows organizations to remain agile, responsive, and competitive, even in the face of unforeseen challenges and opportunities.

Living documents are dynamic planning tools that differ significantly from traditional static plans. They are not set in stone but are expected to change and grow as the situation around the organization evolves. This concept acknowledges the reality that in today's fast-paced world, the only constant is change itself. Therefore, adaptive leaders must embrace the fluidity of their strategic plans, ensuring they can swiftly adjust their course of action when necessary.

One of the key aspects of living documents is their ability to incorporate fresh insights. This involves continuously monitoring the internal and external environment for signals of change, including technological advancements, market trends, regulatory shifts, and competitive actions. Adaptive leaders encourage a culture of curiosity and learning, where team members at all levels are attuned to possible changes on the horizon that could impact the organization and are empowered to contribute their observations and insights.

As new information comes to light, living documents provide a framework for integrating these insights into the organization's strategic direction. This may involve revisiting and revising goals, tactics, and resource allocations to better align with the current landscape. It requires leaders to be decisively proactive, making informed adjustments to strategies and operations before minor shifts turn into significant challenges or missed opportunities.

The ultimate value of living documents lies in their ability to enable quick pivots. In an era where delays can lead to lost opportunities or heightened risks, the agility afforded by these adaptive plans is invaluable. By having mechanisms in place that allow for rapid

79

reassessment and realignment, organizations can seize emerging opportunities, mitigate threats, and maintain a competitive edge.

The dynamic nature of modern business environments demands that strategies not only respond to current conditions but also anticipate future changes. Living documents facilitate this by fostering a strategic mindset that is both reflective and forward-looking. Adaptive leaders use these plans to guide their organizations through the present while also preparing for the future, ensuring that their strategies are robust enough to withstand volatility and flexible enough to embrace innovation.

Several sectors have exemplified the successful implementation of flexible planning. For instance, technology companies often operate in markets characterized by rapid innovation and change. By adopting living documents as part of their strategic planning process, they codify their ability to iterate on product development rapidly, adjust to consumer demands in real time, and stay ahead of technological curves. Another example can be found in global supply chain management, where companies utilize flexible planning to adapt to geopolitical shifts, changing regulations, and fluctuating market demands, ensuring operational continuity and efficiency.

Developing flexible plans that can accommodate new information and shifting circumstances is not merely a tactical choice but a strategic imperative for adaptive leadership. Living documents emphasize agility, responsiveness, and continuous learning. By adopting this approach, leaders can ensure that their organizations are not only prepared to navigate the complexities of the present but are also poised to capitalize on the opportunities of the future. This dynamic planning process stands as a testament to the power of adaptability in driving organizational success in an ever-changing world.

Summary

Adaptability has become an indispensable quality in today's rapidly evolving world. The continuous shifts in technology, market dynamics, societal norms, and global events present challenges that demand an agile and responsive leadership approach. Adaptive leadership strategies are of profound importance in steering organizations through the multifaceted challenges of modernity.

Adaptive leaders possess a unique blend of resilience, openness to change, and the capacity to inspire and mobilize their teams toward shared goals amidst ambiguity. Their leadership style is characterized by a forward-thinking mindset, a deep-seated empathy that connects them with their team on a human level, and a commitment to fostering a culture that values learning and innovation.

81

Moreover, the practical strategies outlined in this chapter for leading through change are actionable tools that can significantly enhance a leader's effectiveness. By fostering a culture of innovation, encouraging experimentation, and developing flexible planning mechanisms, leaders can cultivate an organizational environment that is not only prepared to face change but is also poised to capitalize on it. These strategies emphasize the importance of creating a supportive atmosphere where team members feel empowered to contribute ideas, take calculated risks, and learn from both successes and setbacks.

Adaptability is a critical necessity that enables leaders and their organizations to navigate the complexities of modern organizational life with confidence and strategic foresight. Embracing adaptability means recognizing that the status quo is no longer sustainable and that the future belongs to those who are prepared to evolve. It is about viewing the challenges of change not as obstacles but as catalysts for growth, innovation, and transformation.

Leaders who embody adaptability ensure that their organizations do more than merely survive in the face of change; they thrive. They turn the inevitable challenges of the evolving global landscape into opportunities for organizational and personal growth. This propels organizations toward not just achieving their current goals but also redefining what is possible, pushing the boundaries of their industries, and setting new standards of excellence.

The journey toward adaptability requires a commitment to continuous learning, openness to new experiences, and a willingness to lead by example through the uncertainties of change. By equipping themselves with the traits of agile leaders and implementing practical strategies for navigating change, leaders can ensure their organizations are well-positioned for success in the ever-changing global landscape. Adaptability is the key to transforming the challenges of today into the achievements of tomorrow, heralding a future where organizations not only adapt to change but lead it.

7.Empowerment

Empowerment within the context of leadership involves creating an environment where individuals are encouraged to take initiative, contribute their ideas, and fully engage with their roles. Empowering your team not only elevates individual performance but also enhances collective productivity and innovation across the organization. Embedding principles of trust and support, leaders cultivate a workspace where challenges are viewed as opportunities for growth, and failure is seen as a stepping stone to success, thereby nurturing a resilient and adaptable workforce. By fostering a culture of ownership, accountability, and creativity today's leaders can catalyze the development of a dynamic and innovative team.

Empowerment, as a pivotal strategy within leadership, hinges on the cultivation of key principles of trust and support. These principles are not just abstract ideals but practical necessities that guide every interaction and decision within the empowered framework.

Trust is the cornerstone of empowerment. It signifies a leader's confidence in the abilities and judgment of their team members, allowing them the freedom to take initiative and make decisions within their scope of work. This trust is not blindly given but developed over time through consistent and positive experiences. It involves a delicate balance between providing guidance and stepping back to allow team members to navigate their own paths. Trust fosters a sense of ownership among team members, as they feel genuinely responsible for the outcomes of their actions, driving them to higher levels of engagement and commitment.

Support, on the other hand, complements trust by ensuring that team members have the resources, guidance, and encouragement they need to succeed. Support from leadership manifests in various forms, from providing the necessary tools and training to offering constructive feedback and mentorship. It also means creating a safe environment where team members can voice concerns, ask questions, and seek help without fear of judgment or reprisal. Support is about enabling team members to grow and develop, equipping them with the skills and confidence to tackle challenges and seize opportunities.

Together, trust and support create a powerful synergy that propels team members toward achieving their full potential. They are the practical mechanisms through which empowerment is actualized within the workplace. Trust provides the freedom to act, while support ensures that action is informed, intentional, and effective. This dynamic duo lays the groundwork for a culture of empowerment, where team members are motivated to contribute their best, innovate, and push the boundaries of what is possible.

In essence, the principles of trust and support are not merely nice-to-have attributes but essential components of a leadership strategy aimed at fostering empowerment. They signal to team members that their contributions are valued, their development is a priority, and their well-being is of utmost importance. By embedding these principles into the fabric of their leadership approach, leaders can cultivate an environment where empowerment thrives, leading to enhanced performance, innovation, and satisfaction across the team.

Empowering team members has a profound impact on the dynamics within a team, leading to several positive outcomes. When team members feel empowered, their intrinsic motivation increases. They take greater pride in their work and are more committed to achieving their goals, driven by a sense of ownership over their projects and contributions. Team members who feel supported in taking risks and exploring new ideas are more likely to develop innovative solutions to challenges and contribute to the team's creative output. Empowered teams often exhibit higher levels of performance. The combination of increased motivation, innovation, and the alignment of tasks with team members' strengths leads to enhanced efficiency, quality of work, and achievement of objectives.

Creating a culture of empowerment requires intentional actions from leaders. Clearly articulating the team's vision and values provides clarity to help individuals align their efforts with the organization's objectives. Fostering an environment where team members are encouraged to take initiative and make decisions reinforces the trust and confidence leaders have in their team members' abilities. Acknowledging the achievements of team members, both individually and as a group boosts morale and reinforces the behaviors and contributions that leaders want to encourage.

Empowerment and Team Dynamics

Empowering team members transforms the very fabric of team dynamics, catalyzing a series of positive outcomes that not only enhance the work environment but also drive the team toward unprecedented levels of success. The ripple effects of empowerment are multifaceted, impacting motivation, innovation, and performance in profound ways.

Empowerment acts as a powerful motivator for team members. When individuals feel that they have control over their work and can make decisions that affect their projects, a deep sense of ownership is cultivated. This ownership is not merely about being accountable for tasks but feeling genuinely invested in the outcomes of their efforts. As a result, team members exhibit heightened levels of intrinsic motivation, finding personal fulfillment and pride in their work. This heightened motivation often translates into a more vigorous commitment to their roles and objectives, pushing individuals to go above and beyond in their contributions to the team's success.

The link between empowerment and innovation is unmistakable. An empowered team is a breeding ground for creative thought and innovative problem-solving. When team members feel that their ideas are valued and that they have the support to pursue new avenues of thought, they are more inclined to think outside the box and challenge the status quo. This openness to risk-taking, underpinned by a supportive leadership structure that encourages exploration, often leads to groundbreaking solutions and advancements. The dynamism fostered by this environment propels the team's creative output, ensuring that the organization remains at the cutting edge of its field.

The culmination of increased motivation and a thriving culture of innovation is a marked enhancement in team performance. Empowered teams, characterized by their motivated members and innovative approaches, tend to outperform their less empowered counterparts. The synergy created by aligning team members' tasks with their strengths and interests maximizes efficiency and productivity, leading to superior quality of work. Furthermore, the autonomy afforded to team members allows for more agile responses to challenges, enhancing the team's ability to meet and exceed objectives. This optimized performance is not just about achieving set goals but about setting new benchmarks for excellence within the organization.

Empowering team members fosters an environment where motivation, innovation, and performance are not just goals to be achieved but natural outcomes of a culture that values and invests in its people. The benefits of such an environment are clear: teams that are empowered are not only more satisfied and cohesive but are also more effective, innovative, and successful. Through empowerment, leaders can unlock the full potential of their teams, propelling their organizations to new heights of achievement and setting a standard for excellence in the modern workplace.

Taking Action

Creating a culture of empowerment within an organization is a deliberate and strategic effort that requires leaders to take specific, intentional actions. These actions are designed to cultivate an environment where team members feel valued, trusted, and motivated to contribute their best.

The foundation of an empowered team lies in the clear articulation of the team's vision and values. Leaders must ensure that every team member understands not only the organization's overarching goals but also how their individual roles contribute to achieving these objectives. This clarity of purpose does more than just align efforts; it imbues team

89

members' work with meaning and significance. For instance, when a team member understands how their project fits into the larger picture, their sense of responsibility and ownership is heightened. Leaders can achieve this through regular and transparent communication, using meetings, newsletters, and informal discussions to reinforce the organization's vision and values continually.

By fostering an environment that promotes autonomy and encourages team members to take initiative and make decisions, leaders instill a sense of trust and confidence in their abilities. This autonomy, however, should be balanced with guidance and support, ensuring team members feel equipped to make informed decisions. For example, a leader might provide the team with a framework for decision-making that includes key considerations and potential impacts, thereby empowering team members to act while ensuring their decisions are aligned with organizational goals. This approach not only accelerates personal growth but also contributes to the team's agility and responsiveness.

Acknowledgment and celebration of success are vital in reinforcing the desired behaviors and contributions within a team. Recognition can take many forms, from public accolades in team meetings to personalized notes of appreciation or performance-based rewards. By celebrating both individual achievements and group successes, leaders create a positive feedback loop that motivates team members to continue striving for excellence. This recognition also highlights the value of each team member's contributions, fostering a sense of belonging and commitment to the team's shared goals.

The link between empowerment and growth is undeniable. When leaders offer team members opportunities for professional development, they not only enhance the individual's skill set but also contribute to the organization's capability as a whole. These opportunities might include training programs, mentorship relationships, cross-functional project assignments, or support for continuing education. By investing in the growth of team members, leaders demonstrate their commitment to the individual's career and personal development, which in turn, cultivates a culture of continuous learning and improvement.

Leaders who actively engage in practices that promote autonomy, alignment with the organization's vision, recognition of achievements, and growth opportunities can unlock the full potential of their teams. These intentional actions serve as the building blocks for an environment where team members feel genuinely empowered to contribute their best, driving success and setting new standards of excellence.

Summary

In the landscape of contemporary leadership, empowerment emerges not merely as a beneficial approach but as an indispensable strategy for cultivating teams that are resilient, creative, and capable of surpassing performance benchmarks. The journey toward genuine empowerment is paved with the principles of trust and unwavering support. The impact of such empowerment on team dynamics is profound, with tangible increases in motivation, innovation, and overall performance serving as a testament to the efficacy of this approach.

The cultivation of ownership and accountability within team members, as facilitated by empowerment, engenders a work culture where individuals are not only committed to the success of their projects but are also invested in the collective success of the team. This shift in perspective fosters a proactive and engaged workforce, eager to take initiative and assume responsibility for outcomes. The resultant increase in motivation is a natural byproduct of this sense of ownership, propelling individuals to exert greater effort and dedication toward their roles.

Moreover, the link between empowerment and innovation is particularly noteworthy. In an empowered environment, team members are encouraged to explore new ideas, challenge conventional approaches, and propose novel solutions to problems. This freedom to

92

experiment and take calculated risks, supported by a leadership that values and encourages such endeavors, becomes a fertile ground for innovation. The creative output generated in such settings not only keeps organizations at the forefront of their industries but also contributes to a vibrant and stimulating work environment.

Performance, too, sees a marked enhancement under the influence of empowerment. Teams characterized by high levels of motivation and innovation invariably exhibit superior performance metrics. The alignment of tasks with individual strengths and interests, a hallmark of empowerment, further optimizes efficiency and productivity. Additionally, the agility afforded by empowered teams enables more responsive and adaptive strategies, enhancing the team's capability to meet and exceed set objectives.

The path to creating dynamic, innovative, and high-performing teams is intrinsically linked to a leader's ability to empower their team members effectively. The principles and strategies discussed herein offer leaders a blueprint for cultivating an environment where empowerment is not just an ideal but a living, breathing reality. By embracing these practices, leaders can ensure their teams not only achieve but exceed their goals, setting new standards of excellence and driving the organization to unparalleled success.

8.Continuous Improvement

Continuous improvement is more than a strategy; it's a mindset that distinguishes exceptional leaders from the merely competent. In the modern business landscape, characterized by rapid technological advances, shifting market demands, and evolving workplace dynamics, it is necessary for leaders to remain not just current but ahead of the curve. The quest for leadership excellence is marked by an unwavering commitment to personal and professional evolution, understanding that the quest for improvement is endless and the potential for growth is limitless.

Continuous improvement is of critical importance for the proactive leader's development. It's a process that demands an openness to introspection, a willingness to confront one's limitations, and the courage to step beyond them. By actively seeking feedback, leaders can gain invaluable insights into their leadership style, identify areas for growth, and develop strategies to address them. Seizing learning opportunities, whether through formal education, professional workshops, or informal learning experiences, allows leaders to expand their knowledge base and acquire new skills. Moreover, dedication to ongoing skill enhancement ensures that leaders can stay relevant and effective in their roles, navigating the complexities of their responsibilities with confidence and foresight.

In an era where change is the only constant, the capacity for continuous improvement becomes not just advantageous but critical for leadership success. By embracing the path of continuous improvement, leaders can ensure that they, and their teams, are not merely surviving in a world of constant change but thriving, transforming challenges into opportunities for growth and innovation.

At the heart of the concept of continuous improvement is the cultivation of a growth mindset—a perspective that views abilities and intelligence as qualities that can be developed and improved upon over time. Leaders who embrace a growth mindset are characterized by their openness to new experiences, curiosity about the world, and an unwavering willingness to learn from both their triumphs and setbacks. This propels them to seek out challenges, persist in the face of obstacles, and view failures not as insurmountable roadblocks but as valuable learning opportunities.

The cultivation of a growth mindset transforms the way challenges are perceived, encourages a proactive approach to learning and development, and fosters an organizational culture that prizes resilience, innovation, and adaptability. By embracing and promoting these tenets, leaders not only enhance their own effectiveness but also

95

inspire their teams to pursue excellence, ensuring that the organization remains dynamic and competitive in an ever-evolving landscape.

The Growth Mindset

Leaders who embody a growth mindset view every experience, be it a success or a failure, as a stepping stone towards greater understanding and capability. This approach is instrumental in fostering an environment of relentless pursuit of knowledge and skill enhancement, encouraging leaders to embrace challenges as opportunities to expand their horizons.

These leaders are distinguished by their openness to new experiences and an insatiable curiosity about the world around them. This openness and curiosity drive them to explore uncharted territories, ask probing questions, and delve deeper into the complexities of their field. It's this exploratory spirit that fuels innovation and creativity, pushing leaders to venture beyond conventional boundaries and discover new solutions to old problems.

Instead of shying away from difficult tasks or situations, leaders with a growth mindset lean into these challenges, viewing them as opportunities to test their skills and expand their knowledge. This persistence, even in the face of obstacles, is what sets these leaders

96

apart, enabling them to navigate through adversity and emerge stronger on the other side. The ability to view failures as learning opportunities rather than signs of incompetence is crucial, as it allows leaders to take calculated risks, learn from the outcomes, and apply these lessons to future endeavors.

Adopting a growth mindset requires some leaders to undergo a significant transformation in how they view their abilities and approach their roles. This shift involves moving away from a fixed mindset, where abilities are seen as innate and immutable, to embracing the potential for continuous growth and development. Such a shift necessitates a conscious effort to challenge and reframe longstanding beliefs about talent and intelligence, fostering a belief in the malleability of one's capacities.

Leaders who successfully make this shift are not only committed to their personal development but also actively seek out opportunities for feedback and improvement. They understand that growth is a perpetual journey, marked by ongoing learning and adaptation. Furthermore, by embodying this growth-oriented approach, leaders serve as powerful role models for their teams, inspiring them to embrace a similar mindset. This collective shift towards a growth mindset within the team amplifies the organization's capacity for innovation, adaptability, and sustained excellence.

97

The journey of continuous improvement is marked by specific, actionable strategies that leaders can employ to enhance their leadership excellence. These strategies can serve as a roadmap for leaders seeking to navigate the complexities of their roles while fostering personal and professional growth:

- **Setting Learning Goals**: Identifying specific, measurable, attainable, relevant, and time-bound (SMART) learning goals provides leaders with a clear direction for their development efforts. These goals could range from enhancing communication skills to mastering new leadership methodologies or understanding emerging industry trends.

- **Seeking Mentorship and Coaching**: Engaging with mentors or coaches who have traversed similar paths can offer invaluable insights and guidance. Mentorship provides a platform for leaders to gain wisdom from experienced professionals, while coaching offers a more personalized approach to identifying strengths, weaknesses, and areas for growth.

- **Engaging in Reflective Practices**: Reflection is a powerful tool for continuous improvement. By regularly taking time to reflect on their experiences, decisions, and outcomes, leaders can gain deeper insights into their leadership style, effectiveness, and areas for improvement. Reflective practices could include

98

journaling, meditation, or structured debrief sessions following significant projects or decisions.

- **Embracing Learning Opportunities**: Leaders should actively seek out and embrace opportunities for learning, whether through formal education, workshops, conferences, or online courses. Staying abreast of the latest leadership theories, industry trends, and technological advancements ensures that leaders remain knowledgeable and relevant in their field.

- **Fostering a Culture of Continuous Learning**: Beyond personal development, effective leaders strive to create an environment that encourages continuous learning among their team members. By promoting a culture that values curiosity, innovation, and professional growth, leaders can elevate the collective capabilities of their team, driving organizational success.

Summary

Continuous improvement underscores the pivotal role of adaptability, perpetual learning, and strategic development in the art and science of leading. This principle offers a dynamic approach that is in harmony with the complexities and rapid transformations characteristic of today's global environment. By wholeheartedly

99

embracing a growth mindset, leaders embark on a path that not only cultivates their personal and professional evolution but also empowers them to navigate the multifaceted challenges of their roles with agility and insight.

The adoption of targeted strategies for development—ranging from seeking constructive feedback to embracing diverse learning opportunities—serves as the groundwork for leaders to fortify their knowledge base and refine their skill set. This proactive engagement in self-improvement ensures that leaders remain at the forefront of leadership practices, equipped with the tools and insights necessary to guide their organizations effectively. Moreover, this dedication to continuous growth fosters a culture of resilience and adaptability, ensuring that leaders can swiftly respond to new challenges and opportunities with confidence.

The impact of a leader's commitment to continuous improvement extends far beyond personal benefit. It acts as a catalyst for cultivating a workplace environment where learning, development, and innovation are not merely encouraged but are foundational to the organization's ethos. This culture of empowerment and growth not only elevates the collective capabilities of the team but also enhances engagement, motivation, and job satisfaction.

Leaders who exercise the attribute of continuous improvement can harness the potential of their teams, leverage emerging opportunities, and mitigate challenges with strategic acumen. Continuous improvement is not just a strategy for enhancing leadership effectiveness; it is a fundamental ethos that shapes the very essence of dynamic and successful leadership. By fostering a growth mindset and implementing focused strategies for personal and professional development, leaders can ensure their relevance, impact, and effectiveness in an ever-evolving world. This commitment to perpetual growth and learning sets a powerful example, inspiring teams to embrace the journey of continuous improvement together.

9.Delegation

Effective delegation is a nuanced art that, when executed with precision, significantly amplifies team dynamics, enhances trust, and propels organizational growth. Delegation has a pivotal role in harnessing team members' strengths, fostering trust through the assignment of meaningful responsibilities, and ultimately empowering leaders to dedicate their focus to strategic planning and the overarching vision of the organization.

Effective delegation begins with a leader's ability to recognize and appreciate the unique strengths and capabilities of their team members. This recognition involves a thoughtful assessment of each individual's skills, interests, and potential for growth. By aligning tasks with team members' strengths, leaders not only optimize productivity but also enhance job satisfaction and engagement.

Delegation is inherently an act of trust. By entrusting team members with significant responsibilities, leaders demonstrate their faith in the team's capabilities, thereby fostering a deeper sense of trust within the organization. This trust is twofold; it empowers team members to take ownership of their roles and responsibilities, and it also establishes a foundation of mutual respect and reliability.

Leaders adept in delegating tasks obtain the invaluable benefit of being able to focus on strategic planning and the broader organizational vision. By entrusting operational tasks and responsibilities to their team, leaders can allocate more time and resources to areas where their expertise and vision are most needed, such as developing long-term strategies, exploring new opportunities for growth, and steering the organization through complex challenges.

Additionally, by assigning tasks that challenge team members and encourage them to stretch their capabilities, leaders can foster an environment where continuous learning and development are integral to the organizational culture. This approach not only helps individuals to acquire new skills and knowledge but also prepares them for future leadership roles, ensuring the organization has a robust pipeline of talented, well-rounded leaders.

Strength and Trust

Recognizing team members' strengths goes beyond surface-level appraisal, requiring leaders to delve deep into understanding the unique attributes, skills, and passions that each team member brings to the table. It's about seeing beyond the job description to identify the inherent talents and potential within individuals, a practice that not only enhances the team's overall productivity but also significantly boosts individual job satisfaction and engagement.

Leaders must be actively engaged with their team, paying close attention to how each member approaches tasks, solves problems, and interacts with others. This might involve assessing past performances, soliciting feedback from colleagues, or even directly discussing career aspirations and interests with the team members themselves. Such an in-depth understanding enables leaders to match tasks with the team members best suited for them, ensuring a seamless alignment between individual capabilities and organizational needs.

For instance, consider the delegation of a complex analytical project. By assigning this responsibility to a team member known for their exceptional problem-solving skills and analytical acumen, a leader does more than just allocate a task. They send a clear message of trust and confidence in that individual's abilities, acknowledging their competence and valuing their contribution. This recognition serves as a potent motivator, inspiring the team member to invest their best efforts and further develop their skills. Moreover, it demonstrates to the rest of the team that excellence and hard work are noticed and rewarded, encouraging others to strive for similar recognition.

Aligning tasks with team members' strengths isn't just about efficiency; it's a strategy that fosters a deeper sense of ownership and pride in work. When individuals are given tasks that resonate with their skills and interests, they are more likely to feel personally invested in the outcomes. This investment translates into higher levels of intrinsic motivation, where the drive to excel comes from within. As a result, team members are not only more engaged in their work but are also more willing to go above and beyond to achieve excellence.

Furthermore, this approach to delegation plays a critical role in team members' professional development. By challenging individuals with tasks that stretch their abilities, leaders provide opportunities for growth and learning. This not only helps team members to expand their skill sets but also prepares them for future roles within the organization, contributing to a culture of continuous improvement and advancement.

The act of delegation embodies a leader's confidence in their team's abilities and their commitment to fostering an environment where trust, respect, and accountability are paramount. This approach to leadership not only empowers individuals but also cements the foundation of a cohesive and high-performing team.

At the core of effective delegation lies trust. This trust is not given lightly; it is earned and reinforced through consistent and positive leadership actions. When leaders delegate significant responsibilities to their team members, they are essentially expressing a vote of confidence in those individuals' abilities to handle important tasks and make decisions. This act of faith can significantly boost the team's morale, as it signals to each member that their skills and contributions are valued and trusted.

The delegation of meaningful responsibilities naturally leads to empowerment. Team members who are entrusted with significant tasks feel a sense of ownership over their work, driving them to engage more deeply with their roles. This sense of ownership is empowering; it motivates individuals to take initiative, think creatively, and go beyond the minimum requirements to achieve excellence. The empowerment that comes from delegation also encourages team members to develop their problem-solving and decision-making skills, further enhancing their capability and confidence.

A culture of mutual respect is characterized by open communication, where team members feel comfortable sharing their ideas, challenges, and successes. Moreover, the mutual respect cultivated through effective delegation encourages team members to rely on one another, fostering a sense of camaraderie and teamwork. In such an environment, individuals are more likely to collaborate, offer support, and work together towards common goals.

The willingness to delegate important tasks is also a testament to a leader's commitment to fostering autonomy within the team. Allowing team members the freedom to manage their own projects and make decisions within their areas of responsibility encourages a culture where autonomy is not only desired but expected. This autonomy,

106

however, comes with the expectation of accountability. Shared accountability means that while individuals are responsible for their tasks, the success of these tasks is viewed as a collective effort. This perspective reinforces the notion that every team member plays a critical role in the organization's success, further strengthening the bonds of trust and cooperation within the team.

Recognizing and leveraging the unique strengths of team members not only maximizes productivity and enhances job satisfaction but also fosters an environment where trust, motivation, and growth thrive. Leaders who excel in identifying and nurturing the talents within their teams are better positioned to achieve outstanding results, driving both individual and organizational success.

Building trust through the delegation of responsibility enhances team dynamics, fosters a positive work environment, and drives performance. By demonstrating faith in their team's capabilities, leaders can unlock the full potential of their members, encouraging a culture where empowerment, mutual respect, and shared accountability flourish. In doing so, leaders not only bolster the trust and confidence of their team but also pave the way for sustained success.

Empowering leaders to concentrate on strategic focus through effective delegation allows leaders to transcend day-to-day operational tasks, channeling their energies and expertise into higher-level strategic planning and visioning. Such strategic focus is a necessity in today's fast-paced and complex business environment, where staying ahead requires insightful planning, foresight, and the ability to navigate through multifaceted challenges.

Freeing up bandwidth for strategic focus enables leaders to direct their attention towards the bigger picture, identifying long-term goals and mapping out the pathways to achieve them. This may involve a deep dive into understanding market trends, anticipating future challenges, and seizing opportunities for growth and innovation. When leaders are bogged down by operational tasks, their ability to engage in this kind of high-level thinking is compromised. Effective delegation, therefore, becomes a tool not just for task management but for empowering leaders to fulfill their primary role as visionaries and strategists for the organization.

Leaders are often chosen for their roles based on their unique expertise and experiences. Effective delegation allows them to leverage these strengths, applying their knowledge where it can have the most significant impact. For instance, a leader with a background in

108

innovation can focus on developing new product strategies or exploring emerging markets, while a leader skilled in operational efficiency might concentrate on streamlining processes to enhance productivity. By focusing on areas aligned with their strengths, leaders can contribute more effectively to the organization's growth and success.

A strategic focus facilitated by delegation is instrumental in nurturing organizational growth and fostering innovation. Leaders who have the bandwidth to explore new opportunities can guide their organizations into uncharted territories, whether it's through the adoption of cutting-edge technologies, expansion into new markets, or the development of revolutionary products and services. This forward-looking approach is vital for maintaining a competitive edge, ensuring that the organization not only keeps pace with industry trends but sets them.

Leaders with a strategic focus are better equipped to navigate the challenges of modern business, making informed decisions that steer the organization toward stability and growth. Effective delegation ensures that leaders have the mental and temporal resources to devote to crisis management, strategic pivots, and long-term problem-solving, thereby safeguarding the organization against potential threats and leveraging opportunities that arise from change.

Ultimately, effective delegation is crucial for the long-term success and sustainability of the organization. It ensures that leadership

109

energy is concentrated on setting directions, defining visions, and making strategic decisions that will drive the organization forward for years to come. This long-term perspective is essential for building a resilient organization that thrives on continuous improvement, adaptability, and innovation.

Empowering leaders for strategic focus through effective delegation allows leaders to maximize their impact by concentrating on strategic planning and visioning, leveraging their expertise, nurturing growth and innovation, steering through challenges, and ensuring the organization's longevity. By embracing delegation, leaders can unlock their full potential, guiding their teams and organizations towards a prosperous and dynamic future.

Autonomy and Shared Accountability

Encouraging autonomy and shared accountability within a team balances the freedom of individual team members with the collective responsibility towards the team's and organization's objectives. This approach underscores a leader's commitment to not just overseeing tasks but to empowering team members to take charge of their contributions. By delegating meaningful tasks, leaders signal trust in their team members' abilities to manage projects and make critical

110

decisions. This empowerment fosters a work environment ripe for innovation, growth, and a deepened sense of ownership over outcomes.

Creating a culture of autonomy involves more than simply assigning tasks and stepping back. It requires leaders to provide clear expectations, necessary resources, and support systems to enable team members to navigate their responsibilities effectively. Autonomy is cultivated in an atmosphere where team members feel confident in their abilities and clear about their roles. For example, a leader might delegate the coordination of a cross-departmental project to a team member, providing them with the authority to make decisions regarding project timelines, team roles, and workflow processes. This level of autonomy encourages team members to utilize their problem-solving skills, creativity, and initiative.

With autonomy comes the expectation of accountability. In this framework, accountability is not a mechanism for tracking failures but a system for encouraging ownership and responsibility. Leaders who foster shared accountability create an environment where team members understand that while they have the autonomy to make decisions, the outcomes of these decisions impact the team and organization as a whole. This shared sense of responsibility encourages team members to approach their tasks with a higher level of diligence and commitment, knowing that their contributions significantly affect the collective success.

111

Balancing autonomy with shared accountability requires strategic communication and a strong foundational trust within the team. Leaders can facilitate this balance by setting clear goals, providing regular feedback, and encouraging open dialogue about challenges and successes. For instance, regular team meetings where members are encouraged to share updates, challenges, and solutions can foster a sense of collective responsibility and support. Additionally, implementing systems where team members can celebrate successes together and collaboratively address setbacks reinforces the concept of shared accountability.

Trust is built when leaders consistently demonstrate faith in their team members' capabilities and decision-making skills. This trust, coupled with a culture that values cooperation and mutual support, ensures that autonomy does not lead to isolation but rather to a collaborative effort towards common goals. For example, when a team member takes on a challenging project with the autonomy to lead it, the rest of the team remains ready to offer support, advice, and assistance when needed, embodying the essence of shared accountability.

Encouraging autonomy and shared accountability is a dynamic leadership strategy that recognizes the value of empowering team members while maintaining a cohesive focus on the team's objectives. This approach not only enhances individual team members' sense of ownership and responsibility but also strengthens the collective team dynamic, fostering an environment where innovation, productivity, and

112

cooperation thrive. By effectively delegating meaningful tasks and fostering a culture of autonomy balanced with shared accountability, leaders can unlock the full potential of their teams, driving organizational success through the empowered contributions of each team member.

Summary

The art of effective delegation is a fundamental attribute of effective leadership, essential for catalyzing team potential and steering organizations toward their pinnacle of success. Delegation, assumes a critical role in leveraging the unique strengths of team members, cementing trust within teams, liberating leaders to focus on overarching strategic goals, and nurturing an environment conducive to continuous skills development and learning.

The act of delegating is not merely about task distribution; it is a strategic endeavor that requires insight, understanding, and a commitment to the growth of both individuals and the organization as a whole. By acknowledging and utilizing the specific talents and capabilities of team members, leaders can not only enhance the efficiency and effectiveness of their teams but also bolster the

113

confidence and job satisfaction of each individual, creating a more dynamic and engaged workforce.

The foundation of trust laid down through thoughtful delegation acts as a binding force, enhancing the cohesiveness of the team and establishing a robust platform for mutual respect and collaboration. This trust is instrumental in creating a secure environment where team members feel valued and empowered, encouraging them to take ownership of their roles and contribute their best towards the collective success of the organization.

Simultaneously, effective delegation allows leaders to elevate their focus from the minutiae of day-to-day operations to the broader strategic imperatives that drive organizational vision and long-term success. This strategic focus is vital for navigating the complexities of the modern business landscape, identifying new opportunities for growth, and addressing challenges with innovative solutions.

Most importantly, the culture of continuous improvement and skills development fostered through effective delegation is a testament to a leader's dedication to the advancement and well-being of their team. By providing opportunities for professional growth, encouraging learning, and facilitating the acquisition of new skills, leaders can ensure that their teams are not only well-equipped to meet current demands but are also prepared to tackle future challenges.

Masterful delegation stands as a pivotal leadership skill. It empowers teams, optimizes organizational performance, and paves the way for sustained growth and excellence. Leaders who excel in this competency can unlock the full potential of their teams. In doing so, they not only achieve the immediate goals set before them but also contribute to the lasting legacy of their organizations, marked by innovation, resilience, and a steadfast commitment to excellence.

10.Inspiration

Inspiring leadership in others goes far beyond the conventional scope of motivation; it is about kindling a deeper sense of purpose, passion, and potential within each team member. This leadership skill focuses on uplifting individuals to surpass their perceived limitations and achieve exceptional outcomes. Such leaders are adept at creating an environment where team members are not only encouraged to reach their current goals but are also inspired to envision and pursue even greater achievements.

Inspirational leadership embodies the ability to connect with team members on a profound level, fostering a shared sense of purpose and direction. Inspirational leaders excel in painting a compelling vision of the future, one that resonates with the personal aspirations and values of their team. They are storytellers who can articulate the "why" behind the "what," making every task and challenge a stepping stone toward a larger, more meaningful goal. By doing so, they instill a sense of belonging and significance among their team members, driving them to invest not just their skills but their hearts and minds into their work.

Inspirational leaders understand the power of creativity and its role in achieving extraordinary results. They encourage their teams to

116

think creatively, challenge the status quo, and explore new possibilities without the fear of failure. This openness to innovation is crucial for solving complex problems and discovering novel solutions. Inspirational leaders create a safe space for experimentation, where risks are taken, lessons are learned, and creativity flourishes. Through this supportive environment, team members feel empowered to push beyond their limits, exploring new ideas and approaches that drive the team and the organization to remarkable achievements.

Igniting Passion

One of the key attributes of inspirational leadership is the ability to ignite passion and commitment within teams. This involves recognizing and valuing the unique contributions of each team member, creating a culture of appreciation and respect. Inspirational leaders are adept at identifying what motivates each individual. By aligning team members' personal motivations with the organization's objectives, leaders can foster a deeply committed and passionately engaged team.

Igniting hidden passions within your team is a nuanced process that necessitates a leader's commitment to understanding, encouragement, and the facilitation of growth opportunities. This comprehensive approach is pivotal in creating a nurturing environment

117

where team members feel emboldened to delve into and express their passions, even those that might seem unrelated to their immediate job functions.

At the foundation of this process is a thorough understanding of each team member's unique interests, strengths, and aspirations. This understanding can be cultivated through various means such as dedicated one-on-one meetings, engaging team-building activities, and casual, informal conversations. The objective here is to peel back the layers to uncover the driving forces behind each team member's enthusiasm and motivation. Such insights allow leaders to tailor support and opportunities that resonate on a personal level with each team member, thereby fostering a deeper connection and sense of belonging within the team.

Another critical element is the provision of resources and support. This could range from granting access to online courses and workshops to offering time off specifically for personal development purposes. By making such investments in the team's growth, leaders signal a genuine appreciation for their team members' broader professional development and personal interests. This not only empowers individuals to pursue their passions but also reinforces the organization's commitment to nurturing a well-rounded and fulfilled workforce.

Working collaboratively with team members to establish personal and professional goals that resonate with their passions is another effective strategy. This involves fostering a sense of autonomy, allowing individuals to take the lead on projects or tasks that ignite their interests. Autonomy serves as a significant motivator, driving team members to engage more deeply with their work and find satisfaction in the pursuit of their passions. When team members feel they have the freedom to explore and contribute in ways that are meaningful to them, it leads to enhanced engagement, creativity, and productivity.

The impact of such leadership strategies extends far beyond the individual level, contributing to a vibrant, engaged, and innovative team culture. By encouraging team members to explore and integrate their passions into their work, leaders can unlock a wealth of creativity and innovation. This not only leads to increased job satisfaction and engagement but also bolsters the team's cohesion, driving collective success and productivity.

Creating an environment where hidden passions are discovered, nurtured, and celebrated can transform the workplace dynamic, making it more inclusive, dynamic, and productive. Such an approach enhances not just the well-being and satisfaction of individual team members but also fortifies the team's capacity to innovate and excel. Leaders who successfully implement these strategies contribute to building a legacy of empowerment, collaboration, and continuous improvement within their organizations.

119

Conclusion

Truly inspirational leaders stand as paragons of excellence, embodying all of attributes that we have discussed herein. This distinguishes them from their peers and enables them to drive their teams and organizations to remarkable achievements. These leaders not only possess, but exercise daily clarity of vision, effective communication, integrity, empathy, decisiveness, adaptability, a spirit of empowerment, delegation. Each of these attributes does not operate in isolation but intermingles synergistically to forge the quintessential inspirational leader.

Visionary leaders possess the remarkable skill to chart a future path amidst uncertainty, crafting a compelling vision that serves as a beacon, transcending everyday tasks and aligning individual ambitions with the organization's broader goals. This synergy between personal and collective objectives under visionary leadership not only promises organizational success but also fosters personal growth and fulfillment.

Such leadership nurtures an inclusive environment where each contribution is valued, ensuring personal aspirations align with the organization's ambitions, boosting team commitment, and necessitating ongoing adaptability from leaders. The interplay between personal goals and the organizational vision enhances individuals' sense of ownership and motivation, contributing to the collective effort more effectively.

At an organizational level, this shared vision propels the organization towards unparalleled success, with a united team overcoming challenges and driving innovation. Visionary leadership cultivates a collaborative environment ripe for innovation, merging diverse ideas into novel solutions. Ultimately, guided by a unified vision, organizations not only achieve their immediate objectives but also establish a legacy of innovation and excellence, setting new industry standards and fostering a space where innovation and excellence thrive, impacting well beyond their immediate sphere.

The capability of a visionary leader to synchronize individual and collective aspirations under a unified vision is paramount for both organizational success and individual fulfillment. By nurturing a culture that appreciates and integrates the diverse strengths and ambitions of its team, organizations can unleash the full power of their united efforts. This synergy not only advances the organization and its members toward their goals but also forges a lasting legacy of innovation, excellence, and influence. In the art of leadership, clearly communicating a united vision is fundamental, steering both the organization and its members towards a future filled with accomplishments and meaningful contributions.

The effective leader is also an adept communicator. They understand that the essence of leadership lies in the power to convey ideas, expectations, and visions in a manner that resonates deeply with their audience. Through effective communication, these leaders

121

articulate their vision, share knowledge, and instill confidence, ensuring that every team member is informed, engaged, and aligned with the team's objectives.

Effective communication is much more than exchanging information; it's a crucial aspect of impactful leadership, connecting the future's vision with today's realities. Through clear messaging, persuasive intent, active listening, and feedback integration, leaders can foster organizational success and create meaningful workplace connections. The essence of leadership involves conveying a vision that not only guides but also inspires and motivates teams through uncertainty.

Trust, a key component of effective leadership communication, is built on consistent, transparent dialogue and a culture where feedback is both appreciated and applied. This foundation supports robust teams capable of navigating business challenges. Achieving organizational goals relies on leaders' ability to communicate the purpose behind tasks, encouraging team collaboration and innovation. Overcoming communication barriers like differing perceptions and cultural differences highlights the need for leaders to continually improve their communication skills.

Integrity is a guide that ensures actions and words are in sync, laying the foundation for trust and respect within any organization. This alignment between leaders' actions and their declarations forms the ethical backbone of leadership, crucial for fostering an organizational culture rooted in honesty, accountability, and loyalty.

As a guiding force, integrity shapes leaders' decisions toward the long-term benefit of their teams and the organization, building a profound trust that enhances openness and innovation. It also establishes a culture of accountability, where mistakes are part of learning and responsibility is embraced, reinforcing every organization member's commitment to both successes and failures as growth opportunities.

Loyalty, deeply intertwined with integrity, grows from respect for leaders who adhere to their principles, creating a strong sense of belonging and mutual commitment to the organization's vision. Integrity's role is pivotal in shaping an ethical organizational environment, demanding leaders consistently match their deeds with their words to cultivate trust, accountability, and loyalty.

Integrity is essential, driving the ethical standards of an organization and ensuring its success and standing. It involves a steadfast dedication to ethical conduct, promoting a culture that values and practices these principles. Integrity is not just an admirable trait but a lived principle, essential to effective, impactful leadership.

Empathy is crucial, creating an environment where team members feel valued and understood, significantly enhancing both

123

individual and collective performance. This culture of support and inclusivity boosts trust and collaboration, celebrating diverse perspectives and prioritizing well-being.

Developing empathy involves actively listening to understand team members' emotions and perspectives, fostering a sense of belonging. This effort enhances communication and supports personalized growth opportunities, increasing morale, motivation, and productivity. Feedback, when empathetically delivered, motivates excellence.

An empathetic organizational culture encourages open dialogue, peer support, and models emotional intelligence, fostering resilience and innovation. This approach not only improves internal dynamics but also enhances the organization's external reputation, attracting talent and building strong relationships in a socially connected world. Empathetic leadership is essential for cultivating a supportive, inclusive culture that drives success and leaves a lasting, positive impact.

Decisive leadership is grounded in a clear decision-making framework, alignment with organizational values, collaborative environments, critical evaluation of options, making informed choices with confidence, and a commitment to learning from each decision. This approach offers a balanced and adaptable method for decision-making, emphasizing the importance of understanding implications and ensuring decisions align with core values.

Collaboration is key, drawing on diverse perspectives to enhance decision quality and foster a sense of inclusivity. Critical analysis of each option, considering both immediate and long-term effects, distinguishes strategic leadership. Confidence in decisions boosts team trust and respect, while a learning mindset encourages continuous improvement and adaptability.

This strategy not only bolsters leadership effectiveness but also cultivates trust, motivation, and engagement within the workforce, setting the organization on a course for sustained achievement and adaptability in a dynamic global landscape.

Adaptability is crucial in today's fast-changing world, where technological advances, market shifts, and global events demand agile leadership. Adaptive leaders, known for their resilience, openness to change, and ability to inspire teams, foster a culture of learning and innovation. They implement strategies such as promoting innovation, encouraging experimentation, and flexible planning to navigate and capitalize on change, creating an environment where team members are empowered to take risks and learn from outcomes.

Embracing adaptability, leaders recognize the need to evolve beyond the status quo, seeing change as an opportunity for growth and transformation. This mindset not only helps organizations survive but thrive, pushing boundaries and setting new standards in their industries.

125

The path to adaptability involves continuous learning and a readiness to face uncertainty with a proactive approach. By adopting the traits of adaptive leadership and practical change management strategies, leaders can position their organizations for success in a dynamic world. Adaptability is essential for turning today's challenges into tomorrow's achievements, ensuring organizations lead the way in innovation and excellence.

Empowering your team is a crucial component of developing resilient, innovative teams that exceed performance goals. Trust and support are key to genuine empowerment, significantly boosting team motivation, creativity, and performance. Empowerment instills a sense of ownership and accountability in team members, leading to a committed and proactive workforce ready to take initiative and responsibility.

This sense of ownership naturally enhances motivation, pushing individuals to contribute more passionately to their roles. Furthermore, empowerment fosters an environment ripe for innovation, where team members freely explore new ideas and propose creative solutions, keeping organizations competitive and invigorating the workplace. Performance improves as individuals are empowered to utilize their talents and experiences toward a shared goal. Aligning tasks with individual talents enhances efficiency, while empowered teams' agility allows for quicker adaptation to challenges, surpassing objectives.

Effective delegation is crucial for unlocking team potential and guiding organizations to success. It's more than task distribution; it's a strategic effort that leverages team strengths, builds trust, and focuses leaders on strategic goals while promoting skill development. By recognizing team members' talents, leaders boost efficiency, confidence, and engagement, fostering a cohesive, empowered workforce.

Thoughtful delegation enhances team unity and trust, crucial for a collaborative and secure work environment. It also shifts leaders' focus to strategic planning, essential for overcoming business challenges and spurring growth. Moreover, fostering a culture of learning and development through delegation demonstrates a leader's commitment to their team's growth, preparing them for future challenges.

Masterful delegation is key to empowering teams and achieving organizational excellence. Leaders proficient in delegation not only meet immediate objectives but also leave a lasting impact through innovation and resilience, contributing to their organization's legacy.

As we conclude this exploration into the essential attributes of effective, inspirational leadership, we've unraveled the complexities that shape the path to becoming an inspirational leader. This journey reveals a multifaceted tapestry, crafted from the essential threads of vision, communication, integrity, empathy, decisiveness, adaptability, empowerment, and delegation. It's through the meticulous weaving of these attributes, underpinned by deliberate intention and practice, that

127

the archetype of an inspirational leader is formed. Such leaders possess the unique capability to elevate their teams, guiding them through challenges and inspiring them to exceed their own expectations.

This confluence of qualities embodies the quintessence of inspirational leadership. It equips leaders with the tools to not only forge a compelling vision but also to communicate this vision with conviction, to stand firm in their principles, to connect with their team on a profound level, to navigate through uncertainty with decisive action, and to foster an environment where empowerment and collaboration flourish. This comprehensive leadership model transcends mere task management, positioning leaders as catalysts for potential and growth within their teams.

The impact of mastering these attributes extends far beyond achieving temporary goals. Inspirational leaders leave an indelible mark on their organizations, creating a legacy of excellence that not only sets a high bar for performance but also ignites a passion for exceeding it. Their leadership becomes a beacon of inspiration, influencing not just their immediate teams but also the broader organizational fabric and community at large.

Ultimately, leadership is an ongoing adventure of personal and professional evolution, education, and self-discovery. Embracing and refining these foundational attributes enables leaders to unlock both their potential and that of their teams. The culmination of this journey is a leadership legacy marked by significant achievements, innovative breakthroughs, and a lasting influence that motivates individuals and shapes the future of organizations. Inspirational leaders, through their vision, empathy, and unwavering commitment to excellence, pave the way for future leaders, setting a paradigm of leadership that resonates through generations.